W9-DEL-139

HOMOSEXUALITY

**Lesbians and Gay Men
in Society, History and Literature**

This is a volume
in the Arno Press collection

HOMOSEXUALITY

**Lesbians and Gay Men
in Society, History and Literature**

General Editor
JONATHAN KATZ

Editorial Board
Louis Crompton
Barbara Gittings
Dolores Noll
James Steakley

Research Associate
J. Michael Siegelaub

See last pages of this volume
for a complete list of titles

COMING OUT!

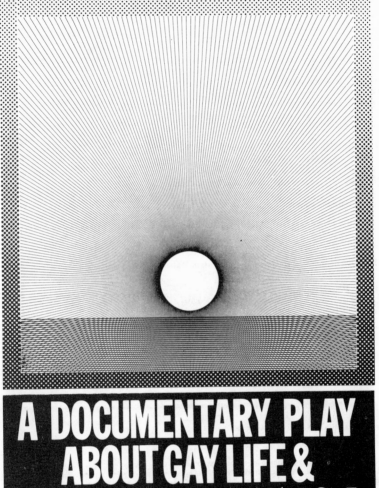

A DOCUMENTARY PLAY ABOUT GAY LIFE & LIBERATION IN THE U.S.A.
by JONATHAN KATZ

ARNO PRESS

A NEW YORK TIMES COMPANY

New York — 1975

MIDDLEBURY COLLEGE LIBRARY

Editorial Supervision: LESLIE PARR

———◆———

First publication 1975 by Arno Press Inc.

The Photographs in this book have been
  reproduced by permission of Bettye Lane and
  Patrick LoBianco.
The musical score has been reproduced by
  permission of Deanna Alida.
The poster is reproduced by permission
  of Louis Fulgoni

HOMOSEXUALITY: Lesbians and Gay Men in
Society, History and Literature
ISBN for complete set: 0-405-07348-8
See last pages of this volume for titles.

Manufactured in the United States of America

———◆———

Library of Congress Cataloging in Publication Data

Katz, Jonathan.
    Coming out : a documentary play about gay life
and liberation in the U. S. A.

    (Homosexuality)
    I. Title. II. Series.
PS3561.A756C6   812'.5'4   75-12327
ISBN 0-405-07399-2

———◆———

Copyright (c) 1972, 1974, 1975 by Jonathan Katz

See individual credits in notes to each scene.

All rights reserved, including the right to reproduce this script or parts thereof in any form. While productions of this play will be encouraged, all dramatic rights in it are fully protected by copyright and no public or private performance or public reading, professional or amateur, may be given without the written permission of the author or his agent. Inquiries should be addressed to the author's representative, Raines and Raines, 244 Madison Ave., N.Y., N.Y. 10016.

The original version of Coming Out! was first presented at the Gay Activists Alliance Firehouse, New York City, on June 16, 1972, directed by David Roggensack. The original cast of five women and five men included Deanna Alida, Blake Berggren, Charlie Brown, Bruce Buchy, Steve Krotz, Michael Lee, Carolyn Nowodzinski, Elizabeth Rosen, Emily Rubin-Weiner, Helen Sandra Weinberg. The Stage Manager was Reed Lenti, the Designers were George James and John Dinsmore. This first version of Coming Out! was produced with the cooperation of the Arts Committee of the Gay Activists Alliance.

Coming Out! is a documentary play adapted from autobiographical and historical accounts, fiction and poetry. The author especially wishes to thank those gay sisters and brothers without whose words there would be no Coming Out!

I also wish to thank E. Carrington Boggan for advice; The New York State Council on the Arts, Volunteer Lawyers for the Arts, and Ronald H. Shechtman for his services; Richard W. Hall for editorial assistance; and Gil Burgos for typsetting.

The title page is from the original poster by Louis Fulgoni.

This play is based on research in gay American history; the author would very much appreciate learning of any additional documented sources. Communications may be sent to his agent or publisher.

For those who first opened the door.

CONTENTS

ACT I

(CAST OF TEN, FIVE FEMALES, FIVE MALES, ENTER AND TAKE SEATS ON TEN BOXES SET IN A STRAIGHT

LINE ACROSS BACK OF STAGE. LIGHTS UP ON STAGE, DOWN IN HOUSE. SPEAKER I STANDS CENTER)

PROLOGUE: THE STONEWALL RESISTANCE, JUNE 27-29, 1969.

SPEAKER I: The Village Voice, 1969. [1]

        This weekend
        the sudden specter
        of "gay power"
        erected its brazen head
        in Greenwich Village
        and spat out
        a fairy tale
        the likes of which
        the area has never seen.

        The forces of faggotry
        spurred by a Friday night police raid
        on one of the city's largest,
        most popular
        gay bars,
        the Stonewall Inn,
        rallied in an unprecedented protest
        against the raid
        and continued to assert
        presence
        possibility,
        and pride
        until the early hours of Monday morning.

SPEAKER II: Friday, June 27th,
        cops entered the Stonewall
        just before midnight.

        (POLICE WHISTLE. TWO COPS RUN UP THROUGH AUDIENCE AND STAND HOLDING

        CLUBS, ONE STAGE L., ONE STAGE R.)

        As the patrons trapped inside
        were released one by one
        a crowd started to gather on the street.

GAY I: I'm a faggot,
        and I'm proud of it!

GAY II: Gay Power!

GAY III: Liberate Christopher Street!

SPEAKER I: Suddenly the paddywagon arrived.

(CAST MAKES SIREN SOUND. THREE QUEENS STAND AND CAMP DEFIANTLY

AT POLICE, FORMING CHORUS LINE, SINGING)

GAYS:

We are the Stonewall girls,
We wear our hair in curls,
We have no underwear,
We show our pubic hairs.

SPEAKER I:

Three of the more blatant queens —
in full drag —
were loaded inside.

(CATCALLS AND BOOS FROM GAYS)

"DYKE":

Push the paddywagon over!

SPEAKER I:

The next person to come out
was a dyke,
and she put up a struggle.

("DYKE" STANDS ON BOX AND GIVES ENERGETIC "FUCK YOU" SIGN

TO COPS)

At that moment
the scene became explosive.
Limp wrists were forgotten.

GAYS:

Pigs!
Fascist cops!
Police brutality!

SPEAKER II:

Pennies and dimes flew.
Escalate to nickles and quarters.
A bottle.
Another bottle.
A cop   says:

COP:

Let's get inside the Stonewall,
lock ourselves inside,
it's safer.

SPEAKER II:

The shattering of windows.
Voices yelling.
From nowhere
comes an uprooted parking meter———
used as a battering ram
on the Stonewall door.

(GAYS START TO BEAT ON BOXES; SLOWLY INCREASING VOLUME AND

RHYTHM)

The sound
doesn't suggest dancing faggots any more.
It sounds like a powerful rage
bent on vendetta.
The front door is completely open.

It seems inevitable
that the mob will pour in.
The cops take out pistols.
They aim unwavering
at the door.

(COP POINTS CLUB AT GAYS LIKE GUN)

COP: We'll shoot the first motherfucker
that comes through that door!

(BLACKOUT)

SPEAKER II: An arm shoots lighter fluid
through the Stonewall window.

(A GAY STRIKES LARGE MATCH IN THE DARKNESS, HOLDING

IT UP IN FRONT OF HER/HIM)

A flaring match follows.
A cop aims his gun.

(CAST MAKES SOUND OF SIRENS; LIGHTS UP SLOWLY)

He doesn't fire.
The sound of sirens
coincides with the whoosh of flames. (MATCH OUT; LIGHTS UP)
It was that close.
It lasted 45 minutes.

SPEAKER I: Sunday night, June 29th, the Stonewall had reopened.
The scene nearby
was a command performance
for queers.
Steps, curbs, and the park
provided props
for the Sunday fag follies.
Older boys
had strained looks on their faces
and talked in concerned whispers
as they watched
the up-and-coming generation
take being gay
and flaunt it
before the masses.

SPEAKER II: Allen Ginsberg walked by
to see what was happening.

GINSBERG: Gay power!
Isn't that great!
We're one of the largest minorities
in the country.
It's about time
we did something
to assert ourselves.

SPEAKER II: Ginsberg expressed a desire

to visit the Stonewall
and ambled on down the Street
flashing peace signs
and helloing the police.
He lent an umbrella of serenity
to the scene
with his laughter
and quiet commentary
on consciousness
and "gay power" as a new movement.

(CAST HUMS 1969 ROCK SONG UNDER THE FOLLOWING SPEECHES,

DANCING TOGETHER SLOWLY)

I followed him into the Stonewall,
where rock music blared
from speakers all around.
He was immediately
bouncing and dancing
wherever he moved.

He left and I walked east with him.

(CAST'S HUMMING NOW VERY LOW; GINSBERG DOWN STAGE CENTER)

GINSBERG:

You know
the guys there
were so beautiful ———
they've lost that wounded look
that fags all had 10 years ago.

(HUMMING RISES TRIUMPHANTLY IN VOLUME AND

CONTINUES UNTIL STOP SIGNAL)

SCENE 1. COMING OUT!

(STARTING FROM STAGE L. THE CAST INTRODUCE THEMSELVES

TO AUDIENCE, EACH SAYING HER/HIS NAME, WAVING, SMILING,

GLOWERING, WHATEVER. THEN:)

MILLETT:

Kate Millett, 1970. [2]

I'm very glad to be here. . .
It's been kind of a long trip. . .

(WALKS TOWARD AUDIENCE)

I've wanted to be here,
I suppose,
in a surreptitious way
for a long time,
and I was always too chicken. . .
Anyway,
I'm out of the closet.
Here I am.

MILLER:

Merle Miller, 1971. [3]

When I was a child
in Marshalltown, Iowa,
I hated Christmas,
but loved Halloween.
I never wanted to take off the mask;
I wanted to wear it everywhere,
night and day,
always.

(WALKS TOWARD AUDIENCE)

It took me almost 50 years
to come out of the closet,
to stop pretending
to be something I was not.

(CROSSING TO STAGE CENTER)

SCHWARTZ: Joan Schwartz, 1970. [4]

For me
coming out meant an end to sex.
I reject that institution totally.
Sex
is an institution
so totally tied up with the penis
and its goal
that boys assume there must be
some poor substitute
for their noble item.
A lot of people
can't figure out "what we do,"
how we make love
without a penis around
for the final consumation.

Lesbianism has nothing to do with sex.
It's not another way to "do it";
it's a whole other way to have contact.
I sleep with women,
make love with women,
am a woman,
a lesbian.
But I don't have sex with anyone.

Radical lesbian sensuality
is a form
which I myself
am helping to create.
It is not an institution
existing outside of me,
like sex is.
It IS me,
us,
as it comes out of our new consciousness.

(ROBINSON CROSSES TO CENTER STAGE AND STANDS ON

BOX)

ROBINSON:

Marty Robinson, 1971. [5]

I came out when I was 20.
I left my family home,
and matured into homosexuality.

But still there is no rest,
For having stopped hiding from oneself,
one may still be
hiding from the world.
When Miller (INDICATING HIM)
says he is a homosexual,
in public,
it is because he has realized
that one can't escape from oppression
by hiding.
Coming out is not asking for trouble,
it sets a cornerstone
for a fuller self-respect.

Even the most pro-homosexual psychiatrists
are wrong in believing
that homosexuals can be freed
merely by being taught
to accept their homosexuality.
No sanity can be found
until the homosexual rebels
against society's ways.
No homosexual
can find full self-understanding
until he or she begins to perceive
the relationship of gays
to the dominant heterosexual society.
The "cure" for homosexuality
is rebellion.

(HART CROSSES TO STAGE CENTER)

HART:

Lois Hart, 1969. [6]

Yes, here I am, goddamit! (STANDS UP ON BOX)
And as I stand up
and take that breath
I can feel
that being here
is not a static thing.

At first
I was mainly aware of what I didn't want———
to no longer consent
to being the victim———
to throw off every piece of shit
that has held me down until now.
Shit like "dyke,"
"sick,"
"degenerate,"
"non-woman,"
"queer,"
"corruptor of children,"
"unnatural,"

"sinful,"
"damned."

But we are not just existing at a time
when an old, unworkable world is dying,
we are living
as a new world struggles for birth.
So a "Yes" has come into it.
I feel my oneness
with the struggles and groanings
of the entire planet.
I know that I am reaching
for something beyond my own imaginings;
that somehow
without really knowing the goal
I have begun to move toward it.
I have stood up
in this too noisy,
too crowded,
polluted
decaying city
and am taking a look around.
What do I want to do?
It has something to do with sharing,
with caring for myself and others,
with working to transform
my immediate environment
so that it fosters
our growing humanity.
What do I have to work with?
Well, I have a sort of dream,
not a very sophisticated one,
and a few ideas. (LOOKING AROUND HER)
I see that there are
a number of people standing near me.
So here we are
scraping the crud off our psyches
as best we can
and proceeding to get to work.

(McREYNOLDS CROSSES TO CENTER, SITS ON BOX)

McREYNOLDS: David McReynolds, 1969. [7]

Happily for me,
but not so happily
for those groups
with which I am associated,
I am an active,
un-sublimated homosexual;
my private life
entitles me
to something close
to an infinity of prison terms.

I come to your church
to talk to your youth about morality.
I do not find it honest
to let my personal friends
and working associates know
I am queer

while keeping that fact a secret
from those to whom it might matter most deeply
as they seek to evaluate
my advice and counsel————
the youth I urge on to action
against this government.

How do I explain
that I am not sophisticated,
but part of Middle America,
of decent and honest parents
and grandparents
and greatgrandparnets.
That is my universe,
where I was the first born child
on both sides of the family,
destined to be
all those things
which the first child
of two large families
must be,
and becoming instead
pacifist,
socialist,
and queer.

I have to say to you,
the congregation of men and women
that I encounter day by day,
that I will be perfectly happy
to live my sexual life in secret
at such time as it is legal,
but it is impossible for me,
finally,
to continue to play a game
which makes me
a kind of Establishment Queer,
keeping silence in public
because I know I shall be left alone
in private.

(EVANS CROSSES TO CENTER AND STANDS ON BOX IN

BACK OF OTHERS SO THAT HE IS THE TALLEST FIGURE)

EVANS: Arthur Evans, 1970. [8]

Gay people
when they first realize that they're gay,
have a process of "coming out,"
that is,
coming out sexually.
We've extended that
to the political field.
We feel that we have to come out politically,
as a community
which is aware that it is oppressed
and which is a political power bloc
feared by the government.

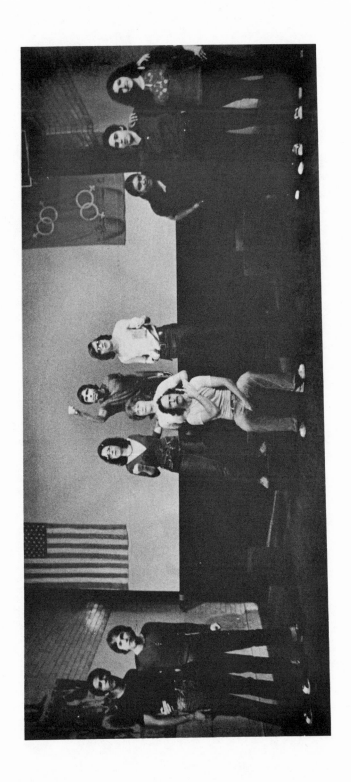

(TWO ACTORS JOIN IN, THE SPEECH INCREASING IN INTENSITY

WITH THE ADDITION OF EACH VOICE)

Until the government is afraid of us——
afraid of our power——
we will never have our rights.

(TWO MORE ACTORS JOIN IN)

The Federal Government
is based on a power structure:
it doesn't matter what the laws say.

(TWO MORE ACTORS JOIN IN)

The Constitution
gives us our rights already.
If that were enough
we'd be a free people today.

(THREE REMAINING ACTORS JOIN IN)

Until we have power
we'll never be free.

(PAUSE. BREAK. ACTORS FORM SEMI-CIRCLE, SITTING ON BOXES

BEHIND ACTOR WHO PLAYED McREYNOLDS, WHO NOW PLAYS

WHITMAN)

WHITMAN: Walt Whitman, 1859. [9]

In paths untrodden,
In the growth by margins of pond-waters,
Escaped from the life that exhibits itself,
From all the standards hitherto published, from the pleasures, profits, conformities,
Which too long I was offering to feed my soul, clear to me that my soul,
That the soul of the man I speak for rejoices in comrades,
Here by myself away from the clank of the world,
Tallying and talked to here by tongues aromatic,
No longer abashed, (for in this secluded spot I can respond as I would not dare elsewhere,)
Strong upon me the life that does not exhibit itself,
                    yet contains all the rest,
Resolved to sing no songs today but those of manly attachment,
Bequeathing hence types of athletic love,
Afternoon this delicious Ninth-month in my forty-first year,
I proceed for all who are or have been young men,
To tell the secret of my nights and days,
To celebrate the need of comrades.

(ACTORS IN BACKGROUND JOIN HANDS)

SCENE 2. UNCLEAN PRACTICES, 1629-1646

(HIGGINSON STANDS)

SPEAKER: Reverend Francis Higginson,
                    Journal, trip to New England

on board the ship Talbot,
1629. [10]

HIGGINSON:

This day June 23rd
we examined
5 beastly sodomitical boys,
who confessed their wickedness
(not to be named).
The fact was so foul
we reserved them
to be punished
by the governor
when we came to New England,
who afterward
sent them back
to be punished in old England,
where they might be hanged
as the crime deserved.

SPEAKER:

John Winthrop,
First Governor
Massachusetts Bay Colony, 1646. [11]

(WALKING BEHIND ACTORS WHO PLAY THE TERRIFIED YOUTH
OF GUILFORD; WINTHROP SEPARATES THEIR HANDS WITH HIS
WALKING STICK)

WINTHROP:

One William Plaine
of Guilford
a married man
being discovered
to have used some unclean practices,
upon examination
it was found
that he had committed sodomy
with two persons in England,
and that he had corrupted
a great part of the youth
of Guilford
by masturbations,
above a hundred times;
and to some who questioned
the lawfulness
of such filthy practice,
he did insinuate
seeds of atheism,
questioning
whether there was a God, etc.
Indeed,
he was a monster
in human shape,
exceeding all human rules
and examples
that ever had been heard of,
and it tended
to the frustrating
of the ordinance of marriage,
and the hindering
the generation of mankind.
The magistrates and elders
did all agree,

and gave diverse reasons
from the word of God,
that he ought to die.
He was executed at New Haven.

SPEAKER: Manhattan Island,
New Netherland Colony,
June 25th, 1646. [12]

(BLACK MALE ACTOR PLAYS CREOLI; STANDS
ON BOX CENTER)

Jan Creoli,
a Negro slave,
guilty
of the crime of sodomy,
this crime being
condemned of God
as an abomination,
the prisoner is sentenced
to be choked to death,
then burnt to ashes.

SPEAKER: Manuel Congo,
a lad ten years old, also a black,
on whom the abominable crime
was committed,
sentenced
to be carried
to Creoli's place of execution
to be there tied to a stake
and faggots piled around him,
for justice sake,
and to be flogged.

(HIGGINSON AND WINTHROP ACTORS RAISE CLUBS TO CREOLI'S NECK

TO CHOKE HIM. BLACKOUT. PAUSE. LIGHTS. MILLER STANDS, CROSSES

DOWN CENTER)

SCENE 3. WORDS!

MILLER: Merle Miller, 1971. [13]

I got my first butch haircut,
just before I started kindergarten.
I was four years old when I started school.
But butch haircut or not,
some boys in the third grade
took one look at me and said,
"Hey, look at the sissy,"
and they started laughing.
It seems to me now
that I heard that word
at least once
five days a week
for the next 13 years,
until I skipped town
and went to the university.

Sissy and all the other words————
pansy,
fairy,
nance,
fruit,
fruitcake,
and less polite epithets.
I did not encounter the word faggot
until I got to Manhattan.

(CROSSES UP CENTER)

I'll tell you this, though.
It's not true,
that saying about sticks and stones;
it's words that break your bones

SPEAKER I: (PLACING BOX IN FRONT OF MILLER, STARTING TO

BUILD PYRE)

Faggot:
a bundle of sticks or twigs
for use as fuel,
1300.
Oxford English Dictionary.

SPEAKER II: (PLACING BOX IN FRONT OF MILLER)

Faggot:
with special reference
to the practice
of burning heretics alive,
especially in phrase
fire and faggot,
and to fry a faggot,
to be burnt alive;
also
to bear, carry a faggot,
as those did who renounced heresy,
1555.
Oxford English Dictionary.

SPEAKER III: (PLACING BOX IN FRONT OF MILLER)

Faggot:
A term of abuse or contempt
applied to a woman,
1591.
Oxford English Dictionary.

SPEAKER IIIA: Faggot:
A male homosexual,
1914.
Oxford English Dictionary.

SPEAKER IV: Fairies,
nances,
swishes,
fags,
lezzes————

	call 'em what you please! 1972. The New York Daily News.
MILLER:	It's words that break your bones.

(STARTING QUIETLY, AND BUILDING UP IN VOLUME AND INTENSITY, UNTIL THE LAST PHRASE; EACH DEROGATORY TERM SPOKEN WITH SOME VARIETY OF CONTEMPT, HATRED. THE MILLER ACTOR SPEAKS ALL THE "EQUALS". ON LINE ACTORS STEP FORWARD ON RIGHT FOOT, POINTING WITH RIGHT HAND AT AUDIENCE)

SPEAKER I:	Fag!
MILLER:	equals
SPEAKER II:	Nigger!
MILLER:	equals
SPEAKER III:	Dyke!
MILLER:	equals
SPEAKER IV:	Spik!
MILLER:	equals
SPEAKER V:	Queer!
MILLER:	equals
SPEAKER VI:	Cunt!
MILLER:	equals
SPEAKER VII:	Fairy!
MILLER:	equals
SPEAKER VIII:	Wop!
MILLER:	equals
SPEAKER IX:	Pansy!
MILLER:	equals

(ON LINE ACTORS NOW STEP FORWARD ON LEFT FOOT, POINTING LEFT HAND)

SPEAKER I:	Kike!
MILLER	equals
SPEAKER II:	Pervert!

MILLER:	equals
SPEAKER III:	Chink!
MILLER:	equals
SPEAKER IV:	Fruit!
MILLER:	equals
SPEAKER V:	Gook!
MILLER:	equals
ALL:	Effete Snob!

(ALL DROP ARMS, BREAK. CATHER AND SPEAKERS I AND II IN

UPCOMING SCENES TAKE SEATS, BACKS TO AUDIENCE, WITH

CATHER CENTER)

SCENE 4. MOREAU DE ST. MERY, ABOUT 1795.

SPEAKER I: (TURNING HEAD TO AUDIENCE)

Moreau de St. Méry, about 1795. [14]

(ST. MERY PLAYED BY A FEMALE, APPEARS FROM BEHIND PYRE OF

BOXES: WITH FRENCH MUSTACHE AND ACCENT; UNCTUOUSLY)

ST. MERY: Although in general
one is conscious
of widespread modesty
in Philadelphia (EMPHATICALLY, WITH DISGUST)

the customs
are not particularly pure.

I am going to say something
which is almost unbelievable.
These American women,
without real love
and without passions,
give themselves up
at an early age
to the enjoyment of (WITH GREAT DISGUST)
themselves,
and they are not at all unwilling
to seek unnatural pleasures (WITH EXTREME DISGUST)
with persons of their own sex.

SCENE 5. WILLA CATHER, 1895.

(CATHER AND SPEAKERS I AND II TURN TO FACE FRONT)

CATHER: Willa Cather, 1895. [15]

There is one woman poet
whom all the world calls great,

though of her work
there remains now
only a few disconnected fragments.
If of all the lost riches
we could have one master restored to us
the choice of the world would be
for the lost nine books
of Sappho.
Those broken fragments
have burned themselves
into the consciousness of the world
like fire.
All great poets have wondered at them,
all inferior poets have imitated them.
Twenty centuries
have not cooled the passion in them.
Save for her knowledge of human love
she was unlearned,
save for her perception of beauty
she was blind,
save for the fullness of her passions
she was empty-handed.
She invented
the most wonderfully emotional meter in literature,
the sapphic meter,
with its three full resonant lines,
and that short, sharp one
that comes in like a gasp
when feeling flows too swift for speech.
Her lyre
responded only to a song of love.
Sappho wrote only of one theme,
sang it,
laughed it,
sighed it,
wept it,
sobbed it.

(CATHER EXITS WITH BOX. SPEAKERS I AND II, FEMALES,

MOVE SEATS TOGETHER)

WILLA CATHER AND ISABELLE McCLUNG. 16

SPEAKER I

One night
back-stage
at the Pittsburgh Stock Company theater,
during the 1898 season,
Willa Cather,
reporter for the Pittsburgh Leader,
met
beautiful
Isabelle McClung,
strong-willed,
art and artist-loving,
rebellious daughter
of wealthy,
conservative,
Judge Samuel A. McClung.

SPEAKER II: The friendship
                  that began that night
                  grew to be a great love.

SPEAKER I: Isabelle invited Willa
                  to share her room
                  and to fix an attic studio
                  in the elegant McClung mansion
                  at 1180 Murray Hill Avenue
                  in the fashionable East End of Pittsburgh.

SPEAKER II: Judge and Mrs. McClung
                  at first pondered the propriety
                  of Miss Cather
                  residing in their house.

SPEAKER I: The daughter, Isabelle
                  promptly threatened
                  to leave home
                  if she could not have her way;
                  Judge and Mrs. McClung relented:
                  Miss Cather could come to stay——
                  temporarily.

SPEAKER II: Willa lived with Isabelle
                  in the McClung mansion
                  until she left Pittsburgh
                  more than five years later.

                  (RISE, CROSSES TO STAGE RIGHT)

SPEAKER I: The two young women
                  would foresake the family group
                  soon after dinner,
                  and evening after evening
                  would go upstairs
                  to the bedroom they shared
                  to read together in quiet.

                  This room was at the back of the house
                  and its wide low window
                  looked out on a downward slope
                  across gardens and shaded streets
                  towards the Monongahela River
                  and green hills rising beyond.
                  There were no close neighbors
                  to destroy their sense of privacy.
                  Here the friends
                  spent many happy hours. [17]

SPEAKER II: Years later, in 1916, Isabelle married
                  and an era in Willa's life came to an end.

SPEAKER I: But when Isabelle died in 1938,
                  Willa did not think
                  she could go on living.
                  When she had recovered
                  from her grief
                  and reflected on the relationship,
                  she believed that Isabelle
                  had been the one person

for whom all her books
had been written.

All the hundreds of letters
that had passed between the two women
were destroyed.
Of this love
there remains but one short verse.
In 1915
Willa Cather's
Song of the Lark
carried the dedication

SPEAKER II: To Isabelle McClung:

On uplands,
At morning,
The world was young,
the winds were free,
A garden fair,
In that blue desert air,
Its guest invited me to be.

(SPEAKERS I AND II KISS AND EXIT)

SCENE 6. SEYMOUR KRIM - DAVID McREYNOLDS, 1959. [18]

HOMOSEXUAL: (CROSSING DOWN R. TO STRAIGHT AUDIENCE)

We no longer have the energy to hide.
You can't know the strain on a person
in always pretending.

SPEAKER I: (CROSSING DOWN RIGHT)

(FILL IN NUMBER) years ago, in 1959,
Seymour Krim, in The Village Voice,
invented a militant homosexual (POINTING)
who spoke with a prophetic voice.

HOMOSEXUAL: We have been
the great unrecognized minority.
That time is ending.
We want recognition
for our simple human rights,
just like Negroes, Jews,
and women.
For years
homosexuals in this country
have cringed behind
a mask of fear.
Legally
we're criminals,
morally,
we're considered perverted,
psychologically,
we've tortured ourselves.
Courageous gay people
are now beginning to realize
that we are human beings
who must fight

        to gain acceptance
        for what we are———
        not what others
        want us to be.

SPEAKER II: (CROSSING DOWN L.)

        David McReynolds———
        who would first publicly declare
        his own homosexuality in 1969,
        disputed Seymour Krim's essay
        in 1959.

        (CROSSES CENTER, TAKES SEAT ON BOXES WITH OTHER

        ACTORS, FORMING AUDIENCE FOR KRIM AND McREYNOLDS,

        FOCUSING BACK AND FORTH SHARPLY AS EACH SPEAKS)

McREYNOLDS: Krim is off base
        suggesting that queer brigades
        are about to storm
        the citadels of prudery.
        Homosexuals as a group
        aren't going to lead any revolt
        because the last thing they want
        is to get involved
        in any real struggle.
        They just want to be left alone
        to lead their precious lives
        in their presently established
        dainty fashion.

HOMOSEXUAL: Homosexuals
        have submitted too weakly until now
        to judgments from above.
        Many of us
        are no longer willing
        to put up
        with this degrading
        of our personalities.
        Merely to live
        we must assert ourselves
        as homosexuals
        who are proud to be
        what we are.

McREYNOLDS: Krim speaks
        of homosexuals coming out of hiding
        to demand and insist
        on their rights as a group.
        This is nonsense.
        I do not see
        any capacity to revolt
        in "gay society."
        It is a destructive sub-culture
        producing corps
        of clean-shaven,
        fresh-scented zombies
        who eat,

sleep,
walk,
talk,
and are dead.
It is a sub-culture
in which sex is substituted
for real personal relations.
As a sub-culture
it produces nothing of value.

HOMOSEXUAL: When it is given unity
homosexual culture
will be seen as constituting
a unique view of experience,
offering insights to all people.
All the dearly bought insight
that has come out
of a closed-door suffering
which can no longer bear its isolation
will be given to society at large.

McREYNOLDS: The Negro sub-culture
has been and remains
tremendously vital.
But what has homosexual society produced
as a society?
Those writers, poets, and artists
who are homosexual
and who have produced
solid and enduring works of art
have done so
in every case
because they saw themselves
as human beings first
and as homosexuals second.
In every case
where a homosexual
fails to make that basic identification
and tries instead
to produce art
based on his sub-culture,
it is fragile,
brittle,
and cold beyond words.

HOMOSEXUAL: We live in a torn-open age
where each minority
is determined to proclaim itself
as good as
its self-appointed judges.
We homosexuals
will be in the leadership
of this revolt.
We've finally rebelled
against feeling miserable
and almost unworthy to live
because our human nature
can no longer stand it.
Look out
for people whom you have driven
to such an extreme!

Life is too fast and mad today
for us to accept
old-fashioned socially induced suffering.
But accept it or not,
we will force our way
into open society
and you will have to acknowledge us.
From 4 to 7 million American adults———

SPEAKER: 10 million! (RISING ON LINE)

SPEAKER: 20 million! (RISING ON LINE)

ALL: More, more! (RISING)

HOMOSEXUAL: are not going to be treated
like criminals or freaks
because we are no longer going to accept
your evaluation of us.
Baby,
remember my words!

(ACTORS APPLAUD; McREYNOLDS LEFT ALONE AS OTHERS

EXIT IN GROUP)

SCENE 7. SHIRLEY, A BLACK LESBIAN.

SPEAKER: Phyllis Chesler,
Women and Madness,
1972. [19]

(INTRODUCING HER)
Shirley, a black lesbian.

SHIRLEY: You know,
I dreaded even thinking
about the term "lesbian"
and I used to cope . . .
by telling myself
that I was normal,
you understand?
And the only thing
that would take my normality away
would be for me
to have an actual gay experience.
And I. . . used to tell myself
that you're not gay
if you never do it.
So I didn't,
'cause I didn't want nothing
to tread on my sanity. . . .
I was trying to live with myself,
and I went out with fellas
and let them fuck me . . . .
The more they did it,
the worse it got,
and the more I pretended to act normal,
the crazier I got.
And I mean I was going out of my mind.

When my mother died
I just stopped pretending
to be something that I wasn't
because it ain't done much ——
straightness in the world——
and it put my mind at ease,
you better believe it,
and I regained my sanity
which was slowly seeping away from me,
from trying to be ungay
and I am definitely gay.
And I realize
that I am not the sick one.
And, you know,
ask me,
I'm a lesbian, right?
And I don't have to love men
and I don't have to fuck 'em
and I damn sure
don't have to depend on 'em
and that is freedom, honey,
because no matter
how heavy my load, honey,
I'm gonna make it
cause I'm free.
I feel that I am free!

SCENE 8. WITCH HUNT, NEW BRUNSWICK, NEW JERSEY, 1973.

SPEAKER: Arthur Bell, 1973. [20]

SPEAKER: In mid-December,
                           last year,
                           two black men
                           were caught
                           in the men's room
                           of the New Brunswick, New Jersey,
                           railroad station
                           and charged
                           with disorderly conduct.

SPEAKER: committing an indecent
                           lewd,
                           and lascivious act,

SPEAKER: and trespassing
                           on railroad property.

                           (BLACK ACTOR, GORDON STANDS CENTER)

SPEAKER: One of the men
                           is Peter Gordon
                           28,
                           single,
                           an English teacher
                           at the New Brunswick High School,
                           director of the town's Afro Culture Club.

SPEAKER: Pete Gordon
                           has been a pain in the side
                           of the status quo

	for most of his five teaching years in New Brunswick.
SPEAKER:	A radical voice on the inadequacies of the school system, he is also the one teacher who constantly and consciously instills a feeling of black pride in his pupils.
SPEAKER:	For the first time in recent history the use of a man's homosexuality as a weapon to destroy him was also being used to stifle his power as a black leader.

(FOUR BOARD MEMBERS FORM LINE STAGE R.

FACING FRONT)

SPEAKER:	The day after Gordon's arrest four Board of Education members met to decide whether the charges were serious enough to warrant Gordon's suspension.
SPEAKER:	The group unanimously agreed
BOARD MEMBER:	Gordon may immediately return to his teaching job.
SPEAKER:	After the decision to reinstate Gordon someone got to the Mayor, the Mayor put overwhelming pressure on individual members of the Board.
SPEAKER:	The following day another Board of Ed meeting was called, including three members previously absent.

(LINE OF BOARD MEMBERS TURN TOWARD GORDON)

SPEAKER:	Turnabout.
SPEAKER:	The new decision:
BOARD MEMBER:	to suspend Gordon from teaching for a week.
SPEAKER:	The teachers' association met, and unanimously agreed
TEACHER:	Gordon should be reinstated.

(STUDENTS FORM LINE STAGE L., FACING GORDON,

CENTER)

STUDENT:	The school student body held an emergency meeting and voted
STUDENT:	to support Gordon.

STUDENT: Monday came.

STUDENT: School opened without Gordon.

STUDENT: Students refused to go to class.

STUDENT: Police were called.

STUDENT: School was suspended.

STUDENT: On Wednesday classes resumed.
             About 25 black students congregated in the cafeteria
             continuing their protest strike.

SPEAKER: Principal William Hyde appeared.

             (HYDE, A WHITE MAN, STEPS FORWARD OUT

             OF BOARD MEMBERS)

HYDE: You have one minute to go to your classes or be arrested.

STUDENT: Six students challenged the principal.
             All were arrested and held overnight.

GORDON: (WITH HUMILITY AND SADNESS, WORDS MEASURED)

             Pete Gordon.
             This is not conceit.
             It's a fact.
             To still my voice as an educator
             is to still the voice
             of all the black teachers
             in this community.
             They want me out.
             and they'll do it
             any way they can.

WRIGHT: (BLACK)

             George Abraham,
             16 years old,
             student,
             New Brunswick High.

             What Mr. Gordon does is his business.
             It's his life.
             The majority of the students
             knew he was gay,
             but they didn't care.
             He never tried to do anything———
             just educate his students.

             Mr. Gordon was dealing in politics
             in New Brunswick
             and the politicians
             felt he was a threat.
             Last year
             three firebombs
             were discovered
             at his Afro-Culture Club.

They're afraid of violence in this town,
and we black people
don't want any.
But we've got cops in school now
and they're turning it
into a prison.

STUDENT: Pete Gordon remains suspended.
It may be months
before the case
reaches the grand jury.
School this week is quiet.
So is the town.
But somewhere,
just below the surface,
New Brunswick
is stuck with an infection.

GRAHN: (CROSSING DOWN R.)

Judy Grahn, 1970 21

Any form of behavior
that doesn't fit
the image
that television
and the Reader's Digest
believe
the American people should be like
is usually categorized
as either
subnatural
or supernatural.
Lesbians
are subnatural
when they live next door,
and supernatural
when they live in Paris
and write books.

SCENE 9. GERTRUDE STEIN AND ALICE B. TOKLAS.

THOMSON: (CROSSING DOWN L.)

Virgil Thomson, 1971. 2

Ethics-minded
and moralistic
from her intellectual training
and middle-class upbringing,
and long resistant
toward acceptance
of the lesbian vocation
(though indulging,
we presume,
in its practice)
in 1907
Gertrude Stein
relaxed into a home life
with Alice Toklas
that seems to have been

profoundly satisfactory
from the beginning.

ALINSKY: (CROSSING DOWN R.

AS SHE TALKS STEIN AND TOKLAS ACTORS BEGIN LOVINGLY ARRANGING

BOXES INTO A BED, CENTER)

Albertine Alinsky, 1971.

(IN REFERENCE TO THOMSON)

I have been shocked recently
at the flow of
strange ejaculations
concerning Miss Gertrude Stein.
These utterances
refer to supposed evidence
of sexual perversion
in Miss Stein's life and work.
I object to all such innuendos.
Mr. Virgil Thomson confides
that Miss Stein confessed to him
"her complete lack of sexual occasions with any man."
Thomson insists upon
what he calls Miss Stein's "lesbian vocation,"
saying she participated
"we presume in its practice. . ."
Well, such suppositions are unfounded and offensive.
With whom did Miss Stein participate?
With Miss Toklas?
Absurd!
To even think of such a thing!
Miss Toklas was a modest old maid.
Miss Stein, in fact, described Miss Toklas as
an "old maid mermaid,"
not a sexual and seductive female.
I must emphasize——
there is a great difference
between deep, pure friendships,
and overtly sexual connections.

(STEIN AND TOKLAS KISS, THEN WALK UP STAGE HOLDING HANDS, ONE

ON EACH SIDE OF BED)

Miss Stein's and Miss Toklas's 39 year companionship
was cemented only by the glue of friendship.
But sexual perversion,
impossible!

(STEIN AND TOKLAS LIE DOWN ON BED)

THOMSON: "Among all the sexual aberrations,"
said a Frenchman
"chastity remains the most astonishing."
And crediting this poverty of experience
to either Gertrude Stein
or Alice Toklas

seems to me no less "destructive"
than to admit
the lesbian practice
that has long been known
to have characterized their friendship.

(STEIN AND TOKLAS FACE AUDIENCE FROM BED)

TOKLAS: Gertrude Stein,
"The Song of Alice B.",
1921. [23]

STEIN: I caught sight of a splendid Misses. She had hankerchiefs and kisses. She had eyes and yellow

shoes, she had everything to choose and she chose me. In passing through France she wore

a Chinese hat and so did I. In looking at the sun she read a map. And so did I. . . .

In loving a blue sea she had a pain. And so did I. In loving me she of necessity thought first.

And so did I.   How prettily we swim. Not in water. Not on land. But in love. How often

do we need trees and hills. Not often. And how often do we need mountains. Not very often

And how often do we need birds, Not often. . . .   How often do we need a kiss.

Very often. . . .

(THEY KISS)

SCENE 10. WITCH HUNT, BOISE, IDAHO, 1955. [24]

NEWSBOY: (CROSSES DOWN CENTER WITH BOX. CAST FORMS CIRCLE

OF BOXES IN FRONT OF WHICH THEY STAND)

The Boise Daily Times, 1955.

(STANDS ON BOX)

Boise Men Admit Sex Charges!
Immoral Acts involving Teenage Boys!
Infamous Crimes Against Nature!

EDITOR: Monstrous evil here! Crush the monster!

(IN THIS SCENE THE LINES OF THE MAIN "I" CHARACTERS ARE SPOKEN

COLLECTIVELY BY MALES AND FEMALES. ONE MALE ACTOR, HOWEVER, PERFORMS THE <u>ACTIONS</u> OF THE "I" CHARACTER THROUGHOUT, AND SPEAKS SOME OF HIS LINES)

SPEAKER: It all started out as a political thing.

SPEAKER: One group of Boise politicians and businessmen
             was out to get another.

SPEAKER: It was this power elite
             that went after the "queers."

SPEAKER: They didn't realize the panic they were setting loose.

SPEAKER: It was like they struck a match to a haystack.

SPEAKER: You could feel the hysteria in the air.

SPEAKER: When one of the first men arrested
             was sentenced to life imprisonment
             I said

"I"   Jesus Christ almighty,
             I'd better get the hell out of here.

             ("I" TAKES A FEW STEPS DOWNSTAGE, FACES AUDIENCE)

SPEAKER: I left for San Francisco and got a job in a hotel.

SPEAKER: One day as I was doing my work
             the Boise sheriff walked in with a policeman
             and said I was under arrest.

             (SHERIFF AND POLICEMAN STEP DOWNSTAGE TAKING
             POSITIONS ON EACH SIDE OF "I")

SPEAKER: The manager of the hotel was having a fit.

MANAGER: (RUSHING DOWN IN A CIRCLE IN FRONT OF "I")

             Get him out of here! Get him out of here!
             We don't want him around.

SPEAKER: I'd known the sheriff all my life
             and also his wife who'd come with him.

             (SHERIFF ON ONE SIDE, PANTOMIMES DRIVING; "I" IN MIDDLE;
             SHERIFF'S WIFE ON OTHER SIDE)

SPEAKER: The three of us rode in the car together back to Boise.

             (WIFE SMILES UNEASILY AT "I" — THERE IS NO PROPER
             ETIQUETTE FOR THIS SITUATION)

SPEAKER: It was just like three people on a trip.

(*ASTERISK INDICATES THE END OF ONE EPISODE AND START OF

ANOTHER; MAY BE INDICATED ON STAGE BY LIGHTING OR TONE

CHANGE)

SPEAKER: Back in Boise
the sheriff had his instructions
to take me to a house
where the chief investigator
was doing his questioning.

(INVESTIGATOR AND POLICEMAN TAKE POSITIONS ON EITHER

SIDE OF "I")

"I":   They had me there nine hours, at least,
before they'd let me call my attorney.

SPEAKER: They told me they knew I was the leader
of a sex ring preying on teenage boys.

(INVESTIGATOR POKES FINGER AT "I")

"I":   This was just to upset me, and scare me, and get me to talk.

(POLICEMAN POKES FINGER AT "I")

SPEAKER: They played me a tape
of a boy who claimed I'd held a gun on him,
and made him go down on me.

SPEAKER: I said

"I":   That's not true, the whole thing's a lie!

SPEAKER: They asked me to write out a statement to clarify this.

SPEAKER: I wrote telling exactly what happened. . .

SPEAKER: three or four years earlier
this teenage boy had propositioned me
and we had sex.

SPEAKER: I wrote this statement out, but I wouldn't sign it.

"I":   I still hand't seen a lawyer.

SPEAKER: They told me when they finished with me
I could see my lawyer.

SPEAKER: They charged me with this "infamous crime against nature."

*(THE FOLLOWING EPISODE IS SPOKEN ONLY NOT ACTED OUT.

ALL IN CIRCLE)

"I":   I had my hearing postponed a couple of times
because of my father's illness.

SPEAKER: He was operated on
a few weeks after I was brought back to Boise.

SPEAKER: They found out he had cancer.

SPEAKER: He lasted five months.

SPEAKER: He just sort of withered away.

SPEAKER: There was nothing you could do about it.

SPEAKER: I spent most of my time taking care of him.

SPEAKER: My mother would feed him through a tube,
and I would give him morphine shots to keep him going.

SPEAKER: After he died my grandfather had a stroke.

SPEAKER: Maybe this was due to my situation,
maybe to my father's death.

SPEAKER: Then my grandfather died.

"I":   In September I came up for a hearing.

                *

SPEAKER: At first I'd pleaded "not guilty."

SPEAKER: They told me if I pleaded guilty
I'd save them the cost of a trial
and I'd get off lightly.

SPEAKER: So I changed my plea to "guilty." ("I" STEPS FORWARD)

SPEAKER: My attorney told me

ATTORNEY
("MIKE"):   (STEPPING FORWARD, SPEAKING CONFIDENTIALLY TO

"I"; EMPHATICALLY)

When you go in to the judge for sentencing
be sure to act like you're ashamed,
like you're sorry.

SPEAKER: The hearing had progressed rather well.

(JUDGE STANDS ON BOX LOOKING DOWN ON "I")

SPEAKER: Then the judge asked me

JUDGE: Are you sorry now that you have committed this crime?

SPEAKER: I tried to answer simply as I could.

"I":   I don't feel I've committed any crime.
I performed an act which was perfectly natural to me
and to the other party.
I feel I'm being persecuted.

SPEAKER: I'm not known for keeping my mouth shut.

SPEAKER: The judge said

JUDGE: Be that as it may,
I am set here to judge you
because society says you have committed a crime.

"I":   He sentenced me to seven years;
then he suspended the sentence
and gave me three years on probation,
providing I spent the first six months in the county jail.

* (LIGHTS DOWN LOW)

SPEAKER: I had just a month to do in the county jail.

("I" AND ANOTHER MALE EMBRACING, "I"'S BACK TO AUDIENCE)

SPEAKER: One night I was in bed with this kid;
we'd had sex several times before;
he was having a good time.

SPEAKER: Right while I was going down on him

(FLASH BULB GOES OFF AT AUDIENCE)

there was this flash of light.

SPEAKER: A couple of seconds elapsed,
then the other guy in the cell said

CELL MATE: Alright you godamn cocksucker, get out of that bed.

(LIGHTS UP; "I" AND LOVER TURN TOWARD CELL MATE

WHO FACES THEM THREATENINGLY)

SPEAKER: He turned on the light
and stood with a chair in one hand,
and a camera in the other.

SPEAKER: He banged on the door and yelled

CELL MATE: I've got it! Come and get it!

(DEPUTY TAKES CELL MATE AWAY)

SPEAKER: The deputy took the camera and immediately let him out.

SPEAKER: They took me and put me into a solitary confinement cell.

(DEPUTY ESCORTS "I" TO ISOLATION CELL)

SPEAKER: At three or four in the morning
they took me downstairs
and charged me,
and mugged me,
and booked me all over again.

(THREE DEPUTIES SURROUND "I", TAUNTING HIM)

SPEAKER: They rode my ass constantly
about what a degraded, filthy, vile, horrible individual I was.

SPEAKER: and about how they couldn't wait
to get me locked up forever.

* (DEPUTIES LEAVE "I" ALONE. MOTHER AND MIKE

ARRIVE, APPROACH DEPUTY)

SPEAKER: A couple of days later
my mother, and Mike, my lawyer, came to visit me
and the deputy told them

DEPUTY: We're sorry but you can't see him.
We arrested him in his cell for having sex with a trusty.

SPEAKER: The deputy turned to my mother and said

DEPUTY: You'll thank me for this later on;
I've finally taken this burden from your shoulders.
We're going to put him away for the rest of his life.

"I":   My mother hauled off and knocked him clear across the room.

SPEAKER: The deputy threatened to have her arrested for assault and battery.

SPEAKER: My lawyer, Mike, told him

MIKE: If you do you're going to get another one from me.

* (MOTHER AND MIKE JOIN "I")

"I":   When my mother and Mike were let up to see me
they were furious.

MOTHER: Why couldn't you have waited until you got out of here?

MIKE: Didn't you know they were going to try to trap you?

"I":   I figured my troubles were over;
all I was doing was getting out.

MIKE: Well you're not out now.

SPEAKER: My probation was revoked.

"I":   I got 7 years.

SPEAKER: I heaved a big sigh of relief when I heard that
'cause God, I was petrified.

"I":   I thought I'd get 30 years or life.

* ("I" SITS IN CENTER OF CIRCLE; SPEAKERS WALK AROUND

HIM AS THEY SAY THEIR LINES)

SPEAKER: The worst night I ever spent
was the first in the state prison.

SPEAKER: I didn't know what to expect.

SPEAKER: I didn't sleep a wink.

SPEAKER: The next day I started through orientation.

SPEAKER: The first days you're in there
they give you an old shirt
and pants ten sizes too big for you,
and you have to keep holding them up.

SPEAKER: You can't let go or they'll fall to the ground.

"I":   They do this just to humiliate you,
so you know your place.

* (ACTORS FORM "CELL" AROUND "I", THEIR

BACKS TO HIM.)

SPEAKER: For six months I was in a cell by myself,
about a yard wide and a yard deep.

SPEAKER: No toilet;
just a shit pail with disinfectant in it.

SPEAKER: We constructed our own toilet seats for the pails
which we took out and emptied twice a day.

SPEAKER: They loved us so much
they put the TB ward on the deck right below us.

"I":   It didn't make any difference
if the "sexual perverts" got TB.

* ("I" MOVES OUT OF CELL; HE AND ANOTHER MALE ACT

OUT ENCOUNTER)

SPEAKER: As I was going through the chow line
on the third or fourth day
I say this guy handing out silverware.

SPEAKER: He had been a prize fighter.

SPEAKER: He was a beauty.

SPEAKER: I looked at him and he looked at me.

SPEAKER: He looked at me the whole time I was eating.

SPEAKER: When I got outside the mess hall he was waiting.

LARRY: You got any magazines?

"I":   No.

LARRY: OK.

SPEAKER: Later that day

	he brought me a big stack of magazines, and walked away without saying a word.
SPEAKER:	His name was Larry.
"I":	Before the months was up Larry and I found a way to become lovers.

("I" AND LARRY TOUCH HANDS AFFECTIONATELY,

INTIMATELY)

* ("I" MOVES AWAY FROM ALL THE OTHERS ON STAGE)

SPEAKER:	They let me out quietly after 18 months.
SPEAKER:	When we got out we had to leave the state and not return for one year.
SPEAKER:	A lot of the Boise victims left and never came back.
SPEAKER:	They couldn't face their friends, they were so ashamed.
SPEAKER:	Their friends and employers hadn't stood behind them.
SPEAKER:	One friend of mine was particularly upset and degraded by his arrest, even though he was paroled and didn't serve any time.
"I":	When he was released on probation he went down to San Francisco, and in a short time actually drank himself to death.

* ("I" TAKES PLACE IN CIRCLE, FACING AUDIENCE, CENTER)

SPEAKER:	It's not something I like to think about much.
SPEAKER:	I try to put it out of my mind.
"I":	Occasionally I'll be with a group of people, and someone will mention the Boise witch hunt, and I'll just set there quietly and nod to myself.

SCENE 11. A CITY INVINCIBLE.

GRAHN:	Judy Grahn, 1970. [25]
	My last dramatic encounter with rampant anti-lesbianism occurred three years ago.
	I had parked my motorcycle and a drunk-young man, who did not like the way I looked, came up to me and called me a queer;

when I failed to respond,
he broke my nose.

What upset him
was my intrusion
into two of his manly territories;
machinery and action.
I had antagonized him
as a somewhat liberated woman———
capable of acting and thinking
on my own———
that's what he'd been taught
to react violently against.

ROBINSON:

Marty Robinson, 1971. 26

I was too bloody and numb
to realize that my nose had been broken.
Tom, my lover,
had had his jaw dislocated.
All because
we were holding hands,
walking in the Village
and passed by
the wrong group of straight boys.

(WITH GREAT SADNESS)

I felt like telling
the only black guy in that group
that I too
was a member of a minority
that was fighting for its rights,
but they said I was less than a man
and they jumped us.

MALE I:

Walt Whitman, 1860. 27

FEMALE I:

I dreamed in a dream I saw a city invincible to the attacks of the whole rest
of the earth,

MALE II:

a city where all men were like brothers,
I saw them tenderly love each other, I often saw them in numbers
walking in hand;

FEMALE:

I dreamed that was the new city of friends,

MALE I:

Nothing was greater than the quality of robust love – it led the rest,

MALE III:

It was seen every hour in the actions of the men of that city, and in all
their looks and words.

ALL:

I dreamed in a dream I saw a city invincible to the attacks of the whole
rest of the earth! (BLACKOUT)

END OF ACT I

ACT II

SCENE 1. CITY OF ORGIES, 1860-1899.

WHITMAN:

Walt Whitman, 1860. [1]

Once I passed through a populous celebrated city, imprinting on my
    brain for future use its shows, architecture, customs, and traditions.
But now of all that city I remember only the man who wandered with me
    there, for love of me,
Day by day, and night by night, we were together,
All else has long been forgotten by me——I remember, I say, only one rude
    ignorant man who, when I departed, long and long held me by the hand,
    with silent lips, sad and tremulous.

Walt Whitman, 1862. [2]

(STARTING TO CROSS TO MEET "WILSON")

Friday night,
October 11,
met 19 year old
David Wilson
walking up Middaugh street———
works in blacksmith shop,
lives in Hampden street———
slept with me.

(THEY EMBRACE, KISS, LIE DOWN ON BED)

GERMAN:

A German visitor. [3]

Half a year after my return
from the Franco-Prussian war,
in the early 1870's,
I went to North America,
to try my fortune.
There The Unnatural
is more ordinary than it is here;
and I was able to pursue my passions
more openly, with less fear
of punishment.
The Americans revere this cult
exactly as I do,
and I discovered,
in the United States,
that I was always immediately recognized
as a fellow-worshiper.

AMERICAN:

Gay American Informant
of Havelock Ellis,
about 1900. [4]

It is red
that has become
almost a synonym
for sexual inversion,
not only in the minds of inverts themselves,
but in the popular mind.

(GROUP OF "STREET BOYS" ACT OUT ACTION

DESCRIBED)

To wear a red necktie on the street
is to invite remarks from newsboys and others———
remarks that have the practices of inverts
for their theme.
A friend told me once
that when a group of street-boys
caught sight of the red necktie
he was wearing
they sucked their fingers
in imitation of <u>fellatio.</u>

(GROUP OF "MALE PROSTITUTES" SAUNTER SEXILY DOWNSTAGE

IN UNISON)

Male prostitutes
who walk the streets
of Philadelphia and New York
almost invariably
wear red neckties.
It is the badge of all their tribe.

("INVERT" PULLS OUT RED CHIFFON SCARF)

AMERICAN II: American Informant
of Havelobk Ellis,
about 1900.

The great prevalence
of sexual inversion
in American cities
is shown by the wide knowledge
of its existence.
Everyone has seen inverts
and knows what they are.
The public attitude toward them
is generally a negative one———
indifference,
amusement,
contempt.

The world of sexual inverts
is a community distinctly organized———
with words,
customs,
traditions of its own;
and every city
has its numerous meeting-places.
You will rightly infer
that the police know of these places
and endure their existence
for a consideration;
it is not unusual
for the inquiring stranger
to be directed there
by a policeman.

(ACTORS BUILD "DESK" OF BOXES FOR RIIS WHILE

STEFFENS TALKS)

STEFFENS: Lincoln Steffens, late 1890's. [5]

... I used to go out with the other reporters on cases that were useless to my paper but interesting to me. Crime as tragedy and as part of the police system fascinated me... Crime was a business, and criminals had "position" in the world... I soon knew more about it than [Jacob] Riis did, who had been a police reporter for years; I knew more than [Riis's assistant] Max could tell Riis, who hated and would not believe some of the "awful things" he was told... I remember one morning hearing Riis roaring, as he could roar, at Max, who was reporting a police raid on a resort of fairies.

RIIS: "Fairies!"

STEFFENS: Riis shouted, suspicious,

RIIS: "What are fairies?"

STEFFENS: And when Max began to define the word Riis rose up in a rage.

RIIS: "Not so,"

STEFFENS: he cried.

RIIS: "There are no such creatures in this world."

STEFFENS: He threw down his pencil and rushed out of the office. He would not report that raid, and Max had to telephone enough to his paper to protect his chief.

There were fairies; there were all sorts of perverts; and they had a recognized standing in the demi-world; they had their saloons, where they were "protected" by the police for a price. That raid Riis would not report was due to a failure of someone to come through with the regular bit of blackmail...

WERTHER-JUNE: Ralph Werther-Jennie June,
1922. [6]

During the last decade
of the 19th century
the headquarters
for avocational female-impersonators
of the upper and middle classes
was "Paresis Hall."
The nickname arose
because the numerous
full-fledged male visitors
thought the inverts,
who were its main feature,
must be insane
in stooping to female-impersonation.
They understood "paresis"
to be the general medical term
for "insanity."

On one of my earliest visits
to Paresis Hall,
about January, 1895———
I seated myself alone
at one of the tables.

(HE DOES SO, AND THREE "EFFEMINATE" MALES

APPROACH)

In a few minutes,
three short, smooth faced young men
approached
and introduced themselves:

(THE THREE BOW, ETC.)

REEVES: Roland Reeves,

LESCAUT: Manon Lescaut,

PANSY: Prince Pansy.

REEVES: Mr. Werther———
or Jennie June,
as doubtless you prefer
to be addressed———
I have seen you
at the Hotel Comfort, (KNOWINGLY)
but you were always engaged.

A score of us
have formed a little club,
The Cercle Hermaphroditos.
For we need to unite for defense
against the world's bitter persecution.
We care to admit
only extreme types——
such as like to doll themselves up
in feminine finery.
We sympathize with,
but do not care
to be intimate with,
the milder types, (LOOKING OUT INTO AUDIENCE)
some of whom
you see here to-night
even wearing a disgusting beard!
We ourselves
are in the detested trousers
because only just arrived.
We keep our feminine wardrobe
in lockers upstairs
so that our every-day circles
cannot suspect us
of female-impersonation.
For they have
such an irrational horror of it!

(REEVES, LESCAUT, AND PANSY FORM TABLEAU

UPSTAGE CENTER)

WERTHER-JUNE: (TO AUDIENCE)

Paresis Hall
in the late 19th century
bore almost the worst reputation

of any resort
of New York's Underworld.
While I was an habitué
the church and press
carried on such a war
against the resort
that even the "not-care-a-damn" politicians
who ruled little old New York
had finally to stage
a spectacular raid.
After this
the resort,
though continuing in business
(because of political influence),
turned the cold shoulder
on inverts
and tolerated the presence
of none in feminine garb.
The sexually full-fledged
were crying for blood
(of innocents),
as they did
in the days of witch-burning!
The Hall's distinctive clientele
were bitterly hated,
and finally scattered
by the police.

(ACTORS HAVE BUILT "WITNESS STAND" OF BOXES STAGE L,

FROM WHICH WITNESSES TESTIFY. TABLEAU OF "FAIRIES"

UPSTAGE CENTER ONLY MOVES TO FORM ENTRANCE AND

EXIT FOR "WITNESSES")

INVESTIGATOR: Special Committee
of the New York State Assembly,
1899.
First witness:
George P. Hammond, Junior. [7]

HAMMOND: (ENTERING THROUGH "FAIRIES"; PURITANICAL, PRISSY)

I know this place called Paresis Hall,
392 Bowery, near 5th Street. I was there last night
(under your directions). I knew of it before

(TO AUDIENCE; SMUG, SELF-APPROVING)

as an officer of The City Vigilence League.
What we call male degenerates,
fancy gentlemen,
frequent the place,
and it is a nightly occurence that they solicit men
for immoral purposes.
Men solicit men at the tables.
They have one woman who goes there
they call a hermaphrodite.
They have a piano there,
and these fairies or male degenerates,
they sing some songs.
I never had any difficulty getting in,

not the least;
I have been received with open arms.

("FAIRIES" BOW DEEPLY, FORM EXIT WITH "OPEN ARMS")

INVESTIGATOR: Joel S. Harris.

HARRIS: (ENTERING THROUGH "FAIRIES)

I was at Paresis Hall last night,
in the performance of my duty.
I saw and heard
immoral actions and propositions
by degenerates there.
I have heard of it constantly.
I never had any trouble getting in.
You go in off the street
with perfect ease.

("FAIRIES" MOVE DOWNSTAGE AND GROUP THEMSELVES

AROUND HARRIS, IN TAUNTING POSES; THEIR CLOSENESS,

ALTHOUGH UNSEEN, MAKES HIM UNEASY)

These men that conduct themselves there—
well, they act effeminately;
most of them are painted and powdered;
they are called Princess this
and Lady So and So
and the Duchess of Marlboro,
and get up and sing as women,
and dance;
ape the female character;
call each other sisters
and take people out
for immoral purposes.
I have had these propositions made to me,
and made repeatedly.

(THE "FAIRIES" – HARRIS' DEMONS, TEMPTERS, FURIES —

CIRCLE AROUND HIM WILDLY, LAUGHING, TAUNTING, MOCKING,

REACHING OUT TOWARD HIM SUGGESTIVELY, SEDUCTIVELY,

AMOROUSLY, ECHOING HIS AND THE OTHER WITNESS'S WORDS)

FAIRY I: Lady So and So!

FAIRY II: The Duchess of Marlboro!

FAIRY III: Princess This!

FAIRY IV: They welcomed me with open arms!

FAIRY V: With open arms!

FAIRY I: Never any trouble getting in!

AIRY II: I have had these propositions made to me!

AIRY III: Propositions made to me!

AIRY IV: And made repeatedly!

      (WILD LAUGHTER, BLACKOUT)

SCENE 2. THE SNAKE PIT RAID, MARCH 8, 1970. [8]

      (A GROUP OF GAYS FORMS STAGE CENTER AROUND BOXES

      ARRANGED AS SEATS AND STEPS; THE "PIT")

SPEAKER I: (CROSSING DOWN STAGE L.)

      Anonymous,

      (PUTTING ON BIG, DARK SUNGLASSES)

      1970.

      I was at the door
      at the Snake Pit,
      about five A.M.,
      with my lover Schatzy,
      when the raid took place last night.
      The Pit is not Mafia controlled.
      It's run by Schatzy alone,
      and he takes care of everybody.
      He's beautiful people.
      But to operate in the Village
      you have to pay off.
      I can tell you
      down to the last penny
      what Schatzy pays
      and I can tell you
      who he pays,

      (SELF-IMPORTANTLY)

      but I'm not authorized to say that.

      Deputy Inspector Seymour Pine
      of the First Division
      is the guy behind the raids.
      Pine is looking for a reputation.
      He wants to be Chief Inspector.
      Pine said last night
      he was going to close the Village up.
      The precinct
      is riled up about gays.

      (TWO COPS ENTER, ONE GOING DOWNSTAGE L. TO SPEAKER I,

      THE OTHER DOWNSTAGE R. TO SPEAKER II)

      About five A.M.
      a guy showed up
      at the door of the Pit
      with a warrant

He said

COP I: Can I talk to you for a minute?

SPEAKER I: Schatzy stepped outside the door.
They pushed him back
and forced their way in.

(COPS RAISE CLUBS)

SPEAKER II: (DOWNSTAGE R.)

The cops took all the money
from Schatzy's cash register,
and the kids' tips.
They didn't return any of it.
About four hundred dollars.

SPEAKER I: Then they took us away.
Nobody told us about our rights
or why we were being arrested.
Nobody was told a word.
I tried to ask a cop
when they were arresting us,
"What rights do we have?"
and the cop said

COP I: Shut your fucking mouth.

SPEAKER II: We were treated like animals
at the station.
We were all herded into one big room.
There was a shoeshine machine there.
A couple of kids
turned on the machine
and started shining their shoes
and the cops started coming over
and getting mad.
One cop came and called me a faggot.
He said

COP II   You're nothing but a prick!
If you don't get off that machine
I'm going to tear off
both your fucking feet.

SPEAKER II: After the Stonewall riot last summer
they tried to cool it down
for a while,
but they're starting up again.

(DURING THE FOLLOWING SPEECH VINALES BREAKS IN PANIC

FROM GROUP OF GAYS CENTER. VINALES MOVES STAGE R., IS

BLOCKED BY COP, MOVES STAGE L., IS BLOCKED BY COP.

VINALES MOVES UPSTAGE TO STEPS OF BOXES AND CLIMBS

TO TOP BOX IN PANIC)

EAKER I: Diego Vinales was frightened stiff.
              My own opinion is
              he didn't know what was happening.
              He was afraid maybe he'd be put in jail.
              Diego ran up the stairs
              to the second floor
              of the police station
              and tried to jump from the window
              to the other ledge

              (VINALES JUMPS FROM TOP BOX INTO ARMS OF GAYS)

              and didn't make it.

              (GAYS PLACE VINALES ON HIS BACK OVER BOXES,

              AND KNEEL AROUND HIM)

              I was at the window
              right after he landed on the fence spikes.
              The remarks the cops made
              were unbelievable.
              Diego was a faggot,
              they said.
              They used the word faggot
              so many times
              it was unbelievable.
              One cop said to a fireman

OP I: You don't have to hurry
              with that saw,
              he's dead,
              and if he's not,
              he's not going to live long.

EAKER I: One of the kids heard this
              who happened to be a friend of Diego's.
              He started crying
              and screaming out.
              Then the other kids started crying.
              They saw what was happening
              and they were shaken.

EAKER III: (KNEELING BESIDES VINALES)

              What kept us calm,
              what kept us from panicking
              was talking to each other,
              to keep our spirits up.
              We sang.

              (BITTERLY)

              We sang America the Beautiful.
              We sang We Shall Overcome.
              And then we chanted:

              (QUITELY, BUT DETERMINED)

L GAYS: Gay Power, Gay Power, Gay Power.

SPEAKER IV: (KNEELING BESIDE VINALES)

My own head still hurts.
I still hear Diego
crying out in pain,
I hear him moaning
and screaming.
It isn't easy to shake.

(GAYS HELP VINALES SIT UP; THEY EXIT; TWO COPS TAKE

POSITIONS ON EITHER SIDE OF VINALES)

BELL: Arthur Bell.

News from St. Vincent's
was that Diego Vinales
was off the critical list.
Since he was still technically under arrest
and not allowed visitors,
I sneaked into the hospital
with the hope of getting an interview.
The two policemen
didn't see me pass by.

Vinales was startled
to see a stranger.
He seemed to want to talk.
His voice was weak.
He said

VINALES: My visit to the Snake Pit
was my first to a gay bar in New York.
I am grateful for the support
from the gay groups.
I come from Argentina.
I am worried about my chances
of staying in America.

BELL: He admitted his visa had expired===
he was in the country illegally===
and he was terrified
when the police invaded the Snake Pit,
terrified enough
to attempt escape,
terrified enough
to jump from a second-story window.

Vinales was frightened
about deportation.
His lawyer was working on his case,
but the threat of leaving America
kept Vinales awake at night.
I wanted to know why.
Why was it so important
for him to stay?

VINALES: (THIS SPEECH PLAYED FOR ITS SUPERFICIALITY, NOT PATHOS)

Coming to America
is my dream
since I was a little boy.

I dreamed
of having a car in America
and living in a beautiful building.
I wanted to be rich
and happy
with beautiful clothing,
to laugh
and have many friends
and go to parties.
Maybe this will happen someday.
For this hope
I will stay in America.
I will never go back.
I still have my dream.

(HUBER RISES IMMEDIATELY AND STARTS HIS SPEECH, CUTTING INTO ANY

AUDIENCE EMOTIONAL IDENTIFICATION WITH VINALES'S SPEECH; A

DELIBERATE "ALIENATION EFFECT.")

SCENE 3. HORATIO ALGER ACCUSED, 1866.

HUBER:

Richard M. Huber,
The American Idea of Success,
1972. [9]

The "Horatio Alger hero"
symbolized respect
for the self-made man
and faith
in American equality of opportunity.
As a symbol,
it stood for a poor boy
of lower class origins,
with no advantages
except his own sterling character,
who rose to the top
by his own abilities and efforts.
The symbol has been broadened
to include a fervent hymn
to a freedom of enterprise system.

SPEAKER:

Committee of the Unitarian Church,
Brewster, Massachusetts,
1866.

(VINALES ACTOR NOW PLAYS ALGER: STANDS, CIRCLES

AROUND AND ENDS ON "STEPS" CENTER)

Horatio Alger,
who has officiated as our Minister
for about 15 months past
has recently been charged
with gross immorality
and a most heinous crime,
a crime of no less magnitude
than the abominable
and revolting crime

of unnatural familiarity with boys.
The committee sent for Alger

(THE "COMMITTEE" FORMS A CIRCLE, POINTING

ACCUSINGLY AT ALGER)

and to him specified
the charges and evidence
of his guilt
which he neither denied
or attempted to extenuate
but received it
with the apparent calmness
of an old offender———
and hastily left town
on the very next train
for parts unknown.

(ALGER TURNS, WALKS DOWN STEPS AND EXITS)

HUBER: "Parts unknown"
was New York City
where soon after the Civil War
Horatio Alger
began to write his name
into the history
of the American dream.

SCENE 4. LESBIAN FOLK HEROES.

(SPEAKER I CROSSES DOWN STAGE R.   HALL CROSSES

DOWNSTAGE L. TO STAND ON A BOX. THE FOLLOWING

STORIES ARE ACTED OUT IN PANTOMIME BY ONE WOMAN, WHILE

ANOTHER WOMAN NARRATES)

SPEAKER I: The Weekly Scotsmen, 1901. [10]

"Murray Hall"
died in New York
in 1901.
Her real name
was Mary Anderson
and she was born at Govan,
in Scotland.
Early left an orphan,
on the death of her only brother,

(MALE CROSSES DOWN STAGE, GIVES CAP TO HALL)

she put on his clothes
and went to Edinburgh,
working as a man.
Her secret was discovered (HALL TURNS BACK TO AUDIENCE)
during an illness,
and she finally went to America. (HALL STEPS OFF BOX)

She wore clothes
that were always rather too large
in order to hide her form,

(MALE CROSSES TO HALL, HANDS HER COAT, WHICH

SHE PUTS ON)

baggy trousers,
and an overcoat
even in summer.

She lived as a man
for thirty years,
 making money,
and becoming somewhat notorious
as a Tammany politician,
a rather riotous "man about town."

(HALL CROSSES UP TO TWO COUPLES, SLAPS A MALE ON THE

BACK, HARD, SHAKES MEN'S HANDS, KISSES WOMEN'S HANDS)

She associated much
with pretty girls,
and was very jealous of them.

(TWO WOMEN FROM COUPLES TAKE HALL'S ARMS, CROSS DOWN

STAGE CENTER WITH HER. HALL LOOKS BACK AT MEN AS THE

CONQUEROR)

She associated with politicians,
voted in elections,
drank somewhat to excess,
though not heavily,

(TWO MEN JOIN WOMEN AND HALL LEADS A TOAST, HOLDING

UP AN IMAGINARY GLASS)

swore a great deal, (HALL GESTURES SWEARING)
smoked and chewed tobacco, (HALL SMOKES)
sang ribald songs; (SINGS)
could run,
dance, (DANCES)
and fight like a man, (BOXES)
and had divested herself
of every trace of feminine daintiness.

(HALL LOOKS AUDIENCE IN EYE, IN TOUGH POSITION)

She married twice; (HALL UPSTAGE TO WIFE, KISS)
the first marriage
ended in separation, (WIFE TURNS BACK TO AUDIENCE)
but the second marriage (HALL KISSES SECOND WIFE)
seemed to have been happy
for it lasted twenty years.
Her secret
was not discovered til her death

(HALL TURNS BACK TO AUDIENCE)

when it was a complete revelation,
even to her adopted daughter.

(HALL GIVES CAP AND COAT TO PANTOMIMIST IN NEXT

STORY; HALL BECOMES SPEAKER II, CROSSING DOWNSTAGE R)

SPEAKER II: The East Hampton Star, 1897. [11]

("MAIN" STARTS DOWNSTAGE L. TO BOX AND PANTOMIMES

PITCHING HAY)

A woman who loathes the sight of men and dogs,
and hates them both cordially,
is Miss Augusta Main,
a spinster farmer near Berlin, New York.
As she told a justice
who held her to the grand jury in $1000 bail
for committing an assault
on a male neighbor
with intent to kill:

MAIN: (STOPPING WORK; LOOKING UP)

I never sees men or dogs,
but what I aches to kill 'em.

SPEAKER II: Whenever she discovers a man on her premises.

(MAIN SEES MAN)

she drops all her work

(MAIN LEAVES BOX AND ENERGETICALLY ORDERS

MAN AWAY).

MAIN: Git!

SPEAKER II: If when ordered away
the man does not hurry
she pushes him along with a pitchfork

(MAIN DOES SO)

or any other implement that happens to be handy.
As a consequence
the men folk
give her plenty of room.

(MENFOLK IN LINE, IN UNISON MOVE AWAY FROM MAIN

AS SHE WALKS BY)

Myron Beebe, a neighbor,
for a long time dared to cross Miss Main's premises
to get water from a well.

BEEBE: It saved me a long walk, and I took my chances.

SPEAKER II: (BEEBE & MAIN ACT OUT THE FOLLOWING)

A few days ago
while Beebe
was making the usual short cut
to the well,
Miss Main came out of her house
with a big revolver,
and without any parleying,
opened fire on the man.

(ACTORS SAY: "BANG, BANG, BANG, BANG, BANG!")

He ran for dear life,
while the bullets
whistled about his ears.

When he got home
he found
that out of the six shots fired
two had perforated the overalls
which he wore,

(BEEBE EXAMINES CROTCH OF HIS PANTS)

While another
had torn the rim of his hat.

(BEEBE EXAMINES HIS HAT)

Miss Main has,
since she took the farm,

(MAIN PUTS PRODUCE IN WAGON)

performed all the work
on the place
without any male assistance,
and does it well.

(MAIN STARTS HORSE AND WAGON TO MARKET,

SELLS PRODUCE)

She goes to market
with a load of vegetables
every week,
and sells them herself.
Every day

(CURRIES HORSE)

she cleans out the stables,

(DOES SO)

and rubs down the horses.

(DOES SO)

Only in harvest time
does she seek outside help,
and then she hires
strapping young women.

(TABLEAU FOUR STRAPPING YOUNG WOMEN JOIN MAIN; ARMS

AROUND EACH OTHER IN OLD PHOTOGRAPH TABLEAU; ALL SMILE)

SPEAKER III: (WHILE "YOUNG WOMAN" PUTS ON HAT AND COAT AND

CROSSES TO STAND ON BOX DOWNSTAGE L.)

In St. Louis, [12]
in 1909,
the case was brought forward
of a young woman of 22
who had posed as a man
for nine years.
Her masculine career
began at the age of 13
after the Galveston flood
which swept away
all her family.

(SHE REACHES OUT TO HER FAMILY BEING "SWEPT AWAY")

She was saved
and left Texas
dressed as a boy.

(STEPS DOWN FROM BOX, CROSSES UP CENTER)

She worked in livery stables,

(SHE SHOVELS)

in a plow factory,
and as a bill-poster.

(SHE POSTS BILLS)

On coming to St. Louis
in 1902
she made chairs and baskets
at the American Rattan Works,
associating with fellow-workmen
on a footing
of masculine equality.

(SHE CROSSES DOWN CENTER; TWO WORKMEN CROSS TO

EITHER SIDE OF HER. PANTOMIME PRODUCTION LINE,

HAMMERING, ETC. IN UNISON)

One day a workman
noticed the extreme smallness
and dexterity of her hands.

ORKMAN: (WHILE PRODUCTION LINE CONTINUES)

Gee, Bill,
you should have been a girl.

BILL": How do you know I'm not?

(PRODUCTION LINE FREEZES; WORKMEN EXIT UP STAGE)

PEAKER III: In such ways:
her ready wit and good humor
(BILL MIMES PRIDE IN HER "READY WIT")
disarmed suspicion
as to her sex.

She drank, (SHE DRINKS)
She swore, (SHE SWEARS)
she worked as hard as her fellows,
she fished and camped:
she told stories
with the best of them, (SLAPS HER THIGH AT PUNCH LINE)
and she did not flinch
when the talk grew strong.
She even chewed tobacco. (CHEWS AND SPITS)

(TWO WOMEN CROSS DOWN TO HER; SHE CROSSES UP.

KISSES ONE)

Girls began to fall in love
with the good-looking boy
at an early period,
and she frequently boasted
of her feminine conquests;
with one girl
who worshipped her
there was a question of marriage.

(SHE TAKES HAND OF SECOND FEMALE; DROPS IT, SHAKING

HEAD; TAKES UP HEAVY MANUAL LABOR, HAMMERING

POSTS INTO GROUND)

On account of lack of education
she was restricted
to manual labor,
and she often chose hard work.
At one time she became
a boiler-maker's apprentice, (PUTS ON GLOVES)
wielding a hammer (HAMMERING)
and driving in hot rivets.
Here she was very popular
and became local secretary
of the International Brotherhood
of Boiler-makers.

(FOUR WORKMEN CROSS DOWN TO CONGRATULATE HER,

THEN CROSS BACK UP)

In physical development
she was now somewhat of an athlete.
She could outrun any of her friends
on a sprint; (RUNS)
she could kick higher, (KICKS)
play baseball, (BATS)
and throw the ball overhand
like a man, (THROWS)
and she was fond of football.

(PASSES BALL UNDER HER LEGS)

As a wrestler
she could throw
most of the club members.

(SHE SUMMONS MALE TO WRESTLE; ALL MALES JOIN ON ONE

SIDE; ALL FEMALES BEHIND HER, ON HER SIDE; WRESTLING

CONTINUES UNTIL SHE IS THROWN TO GROUND)

Finally,
in a moment of weakness,
she admitted her sex
and returned to the garments
of womanhood.

(BILL BECOMES WELCOMING WOMAN IN NEXT SCENE;

HOUSE LIGHTS ON)

SPEAKER: May 1st, 1970.
                           7:15 P.M.,
                           auditorium,
                           Intermediate School 70,
                           The Congress to Unite Women.

WOMAN: Good evening.
                           Welcome to the Congress to Unite Women.
                           I'm glad to welcome so many of you here tonight
                           to hear our panel discussion. . .

(STAGE AND HOUSE LIGHTS OFF. IN THE DARKNESS:

RUNNING, LAUGHTER, A REBEL YELL, WHISTLE. STAGE

AND HOUSE LIGHTS ON. AUDIENCE SURROUNDED BY

LESBIANS.)

SCENE 5. THE LAVENDER MENACE ZAP, May 1, 1970. [13]

SPEAKER :   The Lavender Menace Zap!

SPEAKER I: Straight women by the millions
                           have been sold the belief
                           they must subordinate themselves
                           to men,
                           accept less pay for equal work,
                           and do all the shit work around the house.

I have met straight women
who would die
to preserve their chains.
I have never met a lesbian
who believed that she
was innately less rational or capable
than a man;
who swallowed one word
of the "women's role" horseshit.

SPEAKER II:
A few years ago
when gay and straight sisters
in Women's Liberation
picketed the 1968 Miss America Pageant,
the most terrible epithet
heaped on our straight sisters
was "lesbian."
The sisters faced hostile audiences
who called them "commies,"
"tramps,"
"bathless," etc.,
and they faced these labels
with equanimity;
but they broke into tears
when they were called lesbians.

SPEAKER III:
What is a lesbian?
A lesbian is the rage of all women
condensed to the point of explosion.
Lesbian is the word,
that holds women in line.
When a woman hears this word
tossed her way
she knows she is stepping out of line.
Lesbian is a label
invented by the Man
to throw at any woman
who dares to be his equal,
who dares to challenge his prerogatives,
who dares to assert
the primacy of her own needs.
For in this sexist society
for a woman to be independent
means she can't be a woman———
she must be a dyke.

Woman and person
are contradictory terms.
For a lesbian is not considered
a "real woman."
Being a "woman"
is to get fucked by a man.

SPEAKER IV:
"Lesbian" is one of the sexual categories
by which men have divided up humanity.
Affixing the label lesbian,
not only to a woman who aspires to be a person,
but to any situation of real love,
real solidarity among women
is a primary form of divisiveness
among us;

it is the debunking scare term
that keeps women
from forming any primary attachments,
groups or associations
among ourselves.

SPEAKER V: Women in the movement
have gone to great lengths
to avoid confrontation
with the issue of lesbianism.
It puts people up-tight.
They are hostile,
evasive,
or try to incorporate it
into some "broader issue."
They would rather not talk about it.
If they have to,
they try to dismiss it
as a "lavender herring."
But it is no side issue.

(THE WOMEN MOVE TO STAGE CENTER; HOUSE LIGHTS

DOWN AND OUT)

SPEAKER I: It is absolutely essential
to the success and fulfillment
of the women's liberation movement
that this issue be dealt with.

SPEAKER II: As long as the label "dyke"
can be used to frighten women
into a less militant stand,
keep her separate from her sisters,
keep her from giving primacy
to anything other than men and family———
then to that extent
she is controlled by the male culture.

SPEAKER III: What is crucial
is that women begin disengaging
from male defined response patterns.

SPEAKER IV: In the privacy of our own psyches,
we must cut those words to the core.

SPEAKER V: For irrespective
of where our love and sexual energies flow,
if we are male-identified in our heads,
we cannot realize
our autonomy as human beings.

ALL: It is the primacy
of women relating to women,
of women creating a new consciousness
of and with each other
which is at the heart of women's liberation.

(BLACKOUT)

SCENE 6. THE CHICAGO CONSPIRACY TRIAL, 1969 [14]

(DEFENSE WITNESS, GINSBERG, AND PROSECUTION LAWYER

TO STAGE CENTER)

LAWYER: (WITH OBVIOUS DISTASTE)

                 Will you please state your full name?

GINSBERG: Allen Ginsberg.

LAWYER: What is your occupation?

GINSBERG: Poet. . .

LAWYER: You wrote a book   of poems called

                 (BOTHERED BY HAVING TO PRONOUNCE THE ABSURD TITLE)

                 Reality Sandwiches,
                 didn't you?

GINSBERG: Yes.

LAWYER: In there,
                 there is a poem called
                 "Love Poem on Theme by Whitman"?

GINSBERG: Yes. . .

LAWYER: After having refreshed your recollection,
                 would you recite that to the jury?

GINSBERG: "Love Poem on Theme by Whitman,"
                 Walt Whitman being
                 our celebrated bard,
                 national prophet.
                 The poem begins
                 with a quotation
                 of a line by Walt Whitman;
                 "I'll go into the bedroom silently
                         and lie down between
                         the bridegroom and the bride."

LAWYER: And your poem?

GINSBERG: those bodies fallen from heaven
                         stretched out waiting naked
                         and restless,
                 arms resting over their eyes in the darkness,
                 bury my face in their shoulders
                         and breasts, breathing their skin,
                 and stroke and kiss neck and mouth
                         and make back be open and known,
                 legs raised up crook'd to receive,
                         cock in the darkness driven
                         tormented and attacking
                 roused up from hole to itching head,
                 bodies locked shuddering naked,
                         hot lips and buttocks
                         screwed into each other. . .

LAWYER: (TO STOP GINSBERG)

Excuse me!

(SARCASTICALLY TO AUDIENCE, TO MOCK GINSBERG)

Would you explain
the religious significance
of that poem?

GINSBERG: (STANDING, ADDRESSING JURY AND SPECTATORS)

As part of our human nature
we have many loves
many of which we deny ourselves.
Whitman said
the reclaiming of those loves
was the only way this nation
could save itself
and become a democratic
and spiritual republic.
        He said
unless there were
an infusion of feeling,———
of tenderness,
fearlessness,
spirituality,
natural sexuality,
of natural delight
in each other's bodies,———
into the hardened
materialistic,
cynical,
life destroying,
clearly competitive,
afraid,
scared,
armoured bodies,
there would be no chance
for spiritual democracy
to take root in America———
he defined that
as an "Adhesiveness,"
a natural tenderness,
flowing between all citizens,
so that we could work together
not as competitive beasts
but as tender lovers and fellows.
He projected physical affection
between citizen and citizen
which would make us function together
as a community
rather than as a nation
"among the fabled damned of nations."

(GINSBERG CROSSES BACK TO BOX CENTER. SITS)

Walt Whitman
is one of my spiritual teachers
and I am following him in this poem,
taking off from a line of his own

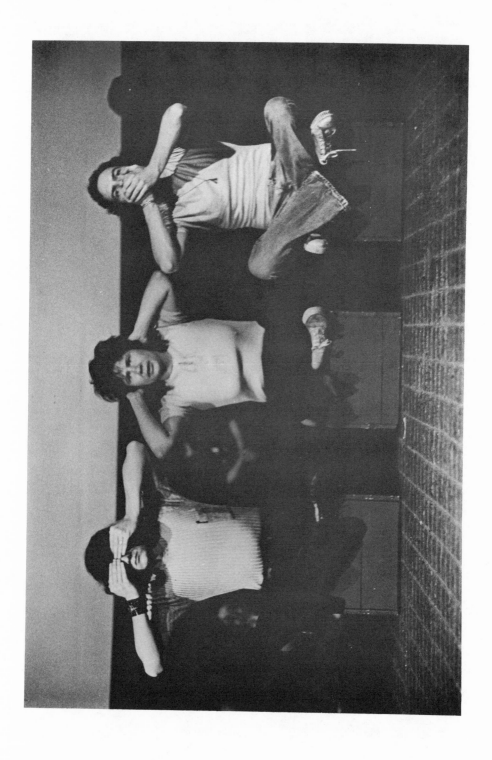

and projecting my own
actual unconcious feelings
of which I don't have shame, sir,
which I feel actually
are basically charming.

LAWYER: (STANDING)

I didn't hear that last word.

GINSBERG: (STANDING)

Charming. . .

(GINSBERG NODS HEAD IN DISMISSAL, EXITS. LAWYER

FOLLOWS)

SCENE 7. NORMAL!

(THREE ACTORS TAKE POSITIONS, SITTING IN A ROW

ON THREE BOXES, LEGS TUCKED UNDER THEM. AT A

SIGNAL THEY TAKE POSITIONS OF THE THREE MONKEYS,

"SEE NO EVIL," "HEAR NO EVIL," "SPEAK NO EVIL.")

SOKOLSKY: (GRADUALLY BECOMING COMPLETELY DERANGED AS

SPEECH PROGRESSES)

ROTH: Sidney Roth, N.Y. Sun, 1943. [15]
The homosexual and bi-sexual person
is an evil
and should be treated as such.
I could fill columns of report and rumor
about this spreading social disease.
It requires stern social treatment.
A liberal interpretation of morals,
"he can't help it,"
"she has a right to her own life,"
must not be tolerated.
Such people are sick
and should be treated by physicians
or institutionalized.

A healthy, building society
does not go in for sex abnormalities.
It is not menaced
by insatiable explorers of new sensations,
the jaded appetites
that find no appeasement
in the love of children
in the companionship of a decent spouse.
Every ancient civilization
decayed and collapsed
because of this particular rot.
It is the end of the greatness
of national existence.
It is evidence

that national masculinity
is being replaced
by the vulgarities of the brothel.
Foul becomes fair in such a climate
not only in morals
but also in politics and economics.
The world becomes bi-sexual;
madmen master the day.

SPEAKER: Time magazine, 1966 [16]

(VENOMOUS)

Even in purely non-religious terms,
homosexuality represents
a misuse of the sexual faculty.
It is a pathetic little second-rate
substitute for reality,
a pitiable flight from life.
As such
it deserves (SWITCH TO "SYMPATHY") fairness,
compassion,
understanding,
and, when possible,
treatment. (BACK TO VENOM)
But it deserves no encouragement,
no glamorization
no rationalization,
no fake status
as minority martyrdom,
no sophistry
about simple differences in taste———
and above all,
no pretense that it is anything
but a pernicious sickness.

DOE: John Doe, 1970.

SPEAKER: (CONFIDENTIALLY, TO AUDIENCE, HAND TO SIDE OF MOUTH)

(a liberal writer
who won't permit a direct quotation.)

DOE: (PEDANTICALLY, "FOR THEIR OWN GOOD")
If I had the power to realize my desire
I would see to it that homosexuals vanish forever
off the face of this earth.
I would expedite this final solution
for the good of the homosexuals themselves,
because they are unhealthy, unhappy misfits,
(ABRUPT SWITCH TO HIS OWN REAL FEELINGS)
and because, personally,
I am totally unable to tolerate them!
(CLAPS HANDS QUICKLY TO MOUTH IN "SPEAK NO EVIL" POSE——
HE HAS SAID TOO MUCH; ALL EXIT.)

SCENE 8. "THE PSYCHOANALYSIS OF EDWARD THE DYKE" BY JUDY GRAHN. [17]

SPEAKER: (CROSSES R. WITH BOX, SITS. EDWARD MAKES COUCH

FROM THREE BOXES: LIES ON THEM. DOCTOR SITS ON BOX

IN BACK OF HER)

Behind the door
which bore the gilt letters
of Dr. Merlin Knox's name,
Edward the Dyke
was lying on the couch.

EDWARD: (SITTING UP)

Four days ago
I went into the powder room
of a department store
and three middle-aged housewives
came in
and thought I was a man.
As soon as I explained to them
that I was really only
a harmless dyke,
the trouble began——

KNOX: You compulsively attacked them.

EDWARD: Oh heavens no,
indeed not.
One of them turned on the water faucet
and tried to drown me.
The other two began screaming
how well did I know Gertrude Stein.
They had my head in the trash can
and were cutting pieces off my shirttail
when luckily
a policeman heard my calls for help
and rushed in.
He was able to divert their attention
by shooting at me,
thus giving me a chance to escape
through the window.

KNOX: (WRITING IN HIS NOTEBOOK)

Apparent suicide attempt
after accosting girls in restrooms.

My child,
have no fear.
You must trust us.
We will cure you of this deadly affliction.
After only four years
of intensive therapy
and two years of anti-intensive therapy,
you'll be exactly the little girl
we've always wanted you to be.

Now tell me briefly
what the word "homosexuality"
means to you,
in your own words.

EDWARD: (CARRIED AWAY BY HER SENSUOUS FANTASIES)

Love flowers pearl
of delighted arms.
Warm and water.
Melting vanilla wafer in the pants.
Pink petals roses
trembling overdew on the lips,
soft and juicy fruit.
Lips chewing oysters.
Pastry.
Gingerbread.
Warm, sweet bread.
Cinnamon toast poetry.
Justice,
equality
higher wages.
Independent angel song.

KNOX:

My dear,
your disease has gotten
completely out of control.
We scientists know of course
that it's a highly pleasurable experience
to take someone's penis or vagina
into your mouth.
But after you've taken
a thousand pleasurable
penises or vaginas
into your mouth
and had a thousand people
take your pleasurable penis or vagina
into their mouth,
what have you accomplished?
What have you got to show for it?
Do you have
a wife
or children
or a husband
or a home
or a trip to Europe?
Do you have a bridge club?
No!
You have only a thousand pleasurable experiences
to show for it.
How sordid and depraved
are these clandestine sexual escapades
in parks and restrooms.

EDWARD:

But sir, but sir,
I don't have sexual escapades
in parks and restrooms.
I don't have a thousand lovers———

KNOX:

Yes. yes.

EDWARD:

She came to me
her slips rustling like cow thieves,
her hair blowing in the wind
like Gabriel.
Lying in my arms

harps play softly.
Oh Bach.
Oh Brahms.
How sweetly we got along
how well we
got the woods pregnant
with canaries and parakeets,
but it only lasted ten years
and she was gone,
poof!
like a puff of wheat.

KNOX: You see the folly
of these brief, physical embraces.
But tell me the results of the experiment
we arranged for you last session.

EDWARD: Oh yes.
My real date.
Well I bought a dress and a girdle
and a squeezy bodice.
I did unspeakable things to my armpits
with a razor.

(ENUMERATING THE FOLLOWING ON HER FINGERS)

I had my hair done,
my face done,
my nails done,
my roast done,
my bellybutton done.

KNOX: And then you felt truly feminine.

EDWARD: And then I felt truly immobilized.
I could no longer run,
walk,
bend,
stoop,
move my arms,
or spread my feet apart.

(THROWS UP ARMS, SLAPS KNEES)

KNOX: Good, good.

EDWARD: Everything went pretty well during dinner.
The worst part came
when we stood up to go.
I rocked back on my heels———
they were three inchers,
raising me to 6 foot 7 inches,
and with all my weight
on those teeny little heels. . .

KNOX: Yes, yes.

EDWARD: I drove the spikes
all the way into the carpet
and could no longer move.
Oh, everyone was nice about it.

My escort offered to call back in the morning.
But my underwear was terribly binding
and the room was hot. . .
so I fainted.

KNOX: (CLEARING HIS THROAT)

It's obvious to me,
young lady,
that this oral eroticism of yours
is definitely rooted in Penis Envy
which showed
when you deliberately castrated your date
by publicly embarrassing him.

EDWARD: (MOANING)

But strawberries.
But lemon cream pie.

KNOX: Narcissism,
Masochism,
Sadism.
Admit you want to kill your mother.

EDWARD: Marshmallow bluebird.

(LIES BACK IN RESIGNMENT)

KNOX: Admit you want to possess your father.
Mother substitute.
Breast suckle.

EDWARD: Graham cracker subway. (SITTING UP)
Pussy willow summer.

KNOX: Admit you have a smegmatic personality.

EDWARD: I am vile!
I am vile!

(THROWS HERSELF BACK ON COUCH)

SPEAKER: Dr. Knox flipped a switch at his elbow

(KNOX FLIPS SWITCH)

and immediately
a picture of a beautiful woman

(EDWARD SITS UP ADMIRING PICTURE)

appeared on a screen over Edward's head.
The doctor pressed another switch (HE DOES SO)
and electric shocks
jolted through her spine.

(ON "SHOCKS" EDWARD JERKS BACK AND SCREAMS IN

EXTREME PAIN)

He pressed another switch, (HE DOES SO)
stopping the flow of electricity. (EDWARD COLLAPSES)
Another switch (KNOX FLIPS SWITCH)
and a photo
of a gigantic erect male organ
flashed into view,

(EDWARD SITS UP, MESMERIZED BY THE VISION)

coated in powdered sugar.
Dr. Knox handed Edward a lollipop.

(SHE MIMES LICKING LOLLIPOP)

EDWARD: I'm saved, I'm saved!

SPEAKER: she said,
tonguing the lollipop.

KNOX: I'm sorry your time is up.

(KNOX SNATCHES THE LOLLIPOP AND SITS)

Leave your check with my secretary.
Come back next week.

(DEFIANTLY; SHE ISN'T COMING BACK)

EDWARD: Yes sir, yes sir,

SPEAKER: Edward said as she went out the door.
In his notebook
Dr. Knox made a quick sketch of his bank.

(BLACKOUT)

SCENE 9. MARCH AND GAY-IN BY JONATHAN KATZ.

(LIGHTS DIM, THEN UP LITTLE BY LITTLE. THE STAGE

IS EMPTY. ONE GAY APPEARS, LOOKING AROUND

APPREHENSIVELY FOR OTHERS. ANOTHER GAY APPEARS;

THEY SHOUT EACH OTHER'S NAMES, EMBRACING HAPPILY,

LAUGHING; THEN ANOTHER AND ANOTHER AND ANOTHER;

NAMES OF EACH CALLED OUT IN GREETING; A SPIRIT OF

JOY, CELEBRATION, AND COMMUNITY. THEN A SPEAKER

BEGINS, AS OTHERS DRAW UP BOXES IN A ROW AND SIT)

SPEAKER: (STANDING ON BOX)

Welcome, welcome,
to the Annual Anniversary
March and Celebration
of the new Gay Liberation Movement

commemorating the Great Battle of 1969
at New York City's
Stonewall Inn.
Here for the first time
raiding police
were confronted
by angry, fighting gays. (GAYS CHEER)
This was the beginning
of a new era
In the gay liberation struggle. (GAYS CHEER)

SPEAKER I: (STANDING)

We start up the Avenue.
Banners wave in the wind.
Tambourines rattle.
Posters advertise our messages. . .

(ON LINE EACH GAY STANDS)

MALE: Gay Power!

FEMALE: Lesbians Unite!

FEMALE: We Are Your Worst Fear
And Your Greatest Fantasy!

MALE: Smash Sexism!

FEMALE: Sappho Was a Right-On Woman!

MALE: Free Oscar Wilde!

FEMALE: A Zap A Day Keeps The Psychiatrist Away.

MALE: Shakespeare Ate Bacon!

MALE: I Am A Homosexual Human Being!

FEMALE: Gay Is Angry!

GAY: Say it loud!

ALL: Gay is proud!

GAY: Say it louder!

ALL: Gay is prouder!

SPEAKER I: The sun is bright yellow
in a clear blue sky. (ALL EXCEPT SPEAKER I SIT)
Police look on blank-faced,
as if we are the most everyday sight.
The sidewalks are jammed with spectators.
Beaming hippie faces.
Unbelieving out-of-town faces.

FEMALE: (RISING, POINTING TO ANOTHER FEMALE MARCHER, WITH

PRIDE)

That's my mother!

(MOTHER WAVES)

SPEAKER II: We pass a man
waving a tattered sign:

OLD MAN: (STANDING; WARNING FINGER POINTING UPWARD)

Sodom and Gomorrah!

SPEAKER II: We ignore him.

SPEAKER III: (STANDING)

At 22nd Street
we pass a ballet studio.
Ballet students in leotards
look down on us
from their seventh floor window.

(DANCER STANDS ON BOX, DOING BALLET EXERCISE

AND WATCHING MARCHERS)

ALL: Join us! Join us!

SPEAKER III: Further uptown
a woman leans out an office window
throwing handfuls of rainbow-hued confetti
in our honor. (FEMALE THROWS CONFETTI)

ALL: Three, five, seven, nine,
Lesbians are mighty fine.

Ho, ho, homosexual,
ruling class is ineffectual.

SPEAKER IV: (STANDING)

We pass a construction site.
Hard hats watch us silently.
Then on a narrow beam
twelve flights up
a worker dances. (DOES SO)
Another waves.
Are they mocking us or applauding?
They seem to smile.
Can it be. . .? (SITS)

SPEAKER V: (STANDING)

42nd Street.
Will it be ugly?
Will some crackpot
take deadly aim at us?

SPEAKER VI: No, we pass in peace.
Alfred joins the parade in his
spangles and gown,
doing his 42nd Street routine.

SPEAKER VII: One marcher yells
      to a 42nd Street hustler:

MARCHER: Don't Sell It, Give It Away!

SPEAKER VII: Further along
      a young gay marcher
      shouts to the spectators:

YOUNG GAY: (FALLING INTO ARMS OF MARCHER NEXT TO HIM)

      Help, help,
      I'm straight and they've kidnapped me!

SPEAKER VIII: (STANDING)

      I look backward and ahead of me.
      I can't see the beginning
      or the end of our march
      there are so many of us.
      Two older gays on the sidewalk watching.
      I smile and motion them to join us.
      They want to
      but are afraid. (SITS)

BYSTANDER: (STANDING)

      I didn't know there were so many of them
      in the whole world.

MARCHER: Honey, you ain't seen nothin' yet!

ALL: Out of the closets and into the streets!

GAY MALE: Out of the streets and into the bushes!

ALL: Out of the bushes and into the streets!

      (ALL EXCEPT SPEAKER IX TURN AND FACE UP STAGE,

      WAVING AND WATCHING THE ONCOMING MARCHERS)

SPEAKER IX: We have reached the park.
      It's been a long, hot walk,
      but we swarm in hundreds
      up the far hill
      then turn to watch the oncoming marchers,
      wave upon wave
      of sisters and brothers,
      multi-bannered and balloon-bearing
      women and men of all descriptions
      are entering the park.

      Where have we all come from?

      (MALE AND FEMALE GAYS ADDRESS GAYS ON STAGE.

      AUDIENCE BECOMES "YOU" STRAIGHTS)

FEMALE I: (STANDING ON BOX)

Today, together,
we have walked with joy
under a blue sky
and a yellow sun.
For too long in the past,
in hiding from you straights,
we were night creatures,
sons of darkness,
daughters of the shadows,
fearful of the light.
For too long
we were strangers in this land,
queer people,
fugitives,
condemned to solitary,
isolated,
exiled,
outlawed,
mocked,
pitied,
denied,
your bastard children
consigned to oblivion.

FEMALE II: (STANDING ON BOX)

For too long,
without protest or resistance,
we accepted it as natural
that your politicians
legislate us criminals,
your police
jail us for our outlawed acts,
your psychiatrists
deny our love legitimacy,
your preachers
condemn us for our sin,
your armies
discharge us with dishonor
(we are not good enough
to maim and kill for freedom),
your employers
fire us,
your bullies
beat us,
your gangs rape us,
your bigots murder us,
your parents disown us,
your comedians mock us,
your liberals tolerate us.
For too long
we accepted all this
as deserved
and natural.

MALE I: (STANDING ON BOX; WITH COMPASSION, NOT ANGER)

For too long,
in the bars,
we eyed each other furtively,
without friendliness.

In the streets
we sniffed
and circled around each other
warily,
waiting.
We met and mated
like dogs in heat.
We bargained for a little contact.
We settled for these brief encounters,
contracted in contempt.
At night
in the darkness of the parks
we gave our bodies
more easily than our names,
we offered ourselves anonymously,
like slaves on the auction block,
like traders in the market place.

MALE III: (STANDING ON BOX; WITH EMPATHY)

With vulture eyes
we looked upon each other hungrily
as meat.
With calculating glance,
with cashiers' hearts,
we toted every score
accounted every number,
had our little tricks.
Street vendors,
we peddled our own flesh,
and sold ourselves too cheap.

FEMALE III: (STANDING ON BOX)

In the past,
defined by others,
lesbians and women,
segregated,
separated,
we were divided from ourselves.
Now,
in our struggle,
we have taught ourselves
to be ourselves,
simply,
strong and gentle
women loving women.
Now,
for the first time
we see clearly
our double-faced oppression,
as females,
as lesbians.
Now we know,
to have our freedom
all sisters must be free.

MALE III: (BLACK)

In the past

unmanned as black,
put down as gay,
enslaved by The Man,
we thought
we had to play the queen
or play the stud.
Now we are in battle
to be ourselves———
liberated men———
sometimes tender,
sometimes tough,
but always
black,
and gay,
and beautiful.

FEMALE IV:

For too long
we have been your laughing stock.
For too long
we laughed with you
and played the fool.
For so long,
for so many of us,
there was something truly unspeakable
about ourselves,
a deep and secret shame.
We wore the mask.
Well, the masks are coming off,
your "freaks"
are coming out fighting,
to face you
in all our "unnatural" beauty.
Like those proud blacks
with their bushy naturals,
we "unnaturals"
are together coming out
to fiercely assert,
and joyfully celebrate
our natures,
fully,
openly,
without shame.

MALE IV:

(STANDING ON BOX)

Our past shame,
we are at last learning,
did not come from out of the blue.
It was your contempt
which we accepted,
internalized,
and made very much our own.
When we have finally realized
that the depth of contempt
in which we have held ourselves
is a true measure
of the depth of hate
in which you hold us,
our anger will be uncheckable,
our actions against you
will burn with rage.

So,
in the words of a new-found comrade,
"Watch your step, honey!"

FEMALE V: (STANDING ON BOX)

In the past
we came to you
quietly,
with the proper air of deference,
begging for acceptance,
toleration,
and a little sympathy.
Well you have missed your chance!
We no longer need your sympathy.
There'll be no more begging,
no more hat in hand.

MALE: We who were invisible
now are walking in the streets
hand in hand,
smiling at each other openly.
At long last,
in public,
proudly,
we dare to speak our name.
No, not speak, shout!
We have been silenced
for too long.

MALE: (STANDING ON BOX)

Together
we will work and shout and fight

FEMALE: until we have our rights,

MALE: until all gay people are free,

FEMALE: until this society is changed!

(SILENCE FOR AS LONG AS IT WILL HOLD, AS CAST STARES

AT AUDIENCE; THEN A SINGLE VOICE SINGS "GAY PEOPLE": 18

"GAY PEOPLE! GAY PEOPLE; WORKING TOGETHER! LOVING

EACH OTHER! SINGIN' IT LOUD! SAYIN' IT PROUD, YOU AIN'T

GONNA KEEP US DOWN"

ALL JOIN IN FOR A REPEAT THEN EXIT.)

END

NOTES

ACT I

1. Adapted from "Gay Power Comes to Sheridan Square" by Lucian Truscott IV, and "Full Moon Over the Stonewall" by Howard Smith, The Village Voice, July 3, 1969. Copyright (c) by The Village Voice and reprinted by permission.

2. Quoted by Merle Miller (see note 3 below). Millett made this coming out speech before the New York Daughters of Bilitis, a lesbian liberation group.

3. Adapted from On Being Different: What It Means to be a Homosexual by Merle Miller. Copyright (c) by Merle Miller and reprinted by permission of Random House Inc. and the author.

4. Adapted from "Some Thoughts after a Gay Woman's Lib Meeting" in Come Out! Dec. - Jan., 1970.

5. Adapted from "Homosexuals & Society: The 'cure' is rebellion" by Marty Robinson, The Village Voice, Ap. 29, 1971. Copyright (c) by The Village Voice and reprinted by permission.

6. Adapted from "Community Center" by Lois Hart, Come Out!, Nov. 14, 1969. Copyright (c) by Come Out! Reprinted by permission of Lois Hart.

7. Adapted from "Notes for a more coherent article" by David McReynolds, Win magazine, Nov. 15, 1969. Reprinted by permission of the author.

8. Quoted in The Gay Militants by Donn Teal, N.Y.: Stein and Day, 1971.

9. "In Paths Untrodden," Leaves of Grass, 1860. Evidence indicates this poem was written in Sept., 1859.

10. Adapted from Higginson's Journal of his voyage to New England. This is available in The Founding of Massachusetts ed. by Stewart Mitchell, Boston: Mass. Historical Society, 1930. The line about "hanging" is added, though factual.

11. Adapted from The History of New England from 1630 to 1649 by John Winthrop, Boston: Little, Brown, 1853. The text indicates Plaine's case took place in 1646.

12. Adapted from Calendar of Dutch Historical Manuscripts in the Office of the Secretary of State, Albany, New York, 1630-1664, ed. by E. B. O'Callaghan, Albany: Weed, Parsons, 1865. I would like to thank Richard George Murray and Louis Crompton for information about this document.

13. (See note 3 above.)

14. Adapted from St. Méry's American Journey, trans. and ed. by Kenneth and Anna M. Roberts, Garden City, N.Y.: Doubleday, 1947. Copyright (c) by the authors and reprinted by permission of Doubleday, Inc.

15. Adapted from "Three Women Poets" (Sappho, Christina Rosetti, Elizabeth Barrett Browning) by Willa Cather, Lincoln, Nebraska Journal, Jan. 13, 1895.

16. This scene, except for speech noted, adapted from material in Willa Cather, Her Life and Art by James Woodress, N.Y.: Pegasus (Bobbs-Merrill), 1970. The exact nature of the relationship between Cather and McClung is unknown. Their story is included here because the existence of close, passionate relations between members of the same sex is of relevance and importance to gay people.

17. Adapted from These Too Were Here: Louise Homer and Willa Cather by Elizabeth Moorhead. Copyright (c) 1950 by the University of Pittsburgh Press and reprinted with permission.

18. Adapted from "Revolt of the Homosexual" by Seymour Krim, The Village Voice March 18, 1959, and "The Gay Underground – A Reply to Mr. Krim" by David McReynolds, The Village Voice, March 25, 1959. Both copyright (c) 1959 by The Village Voice and reprinted by permission.

19. Adapted from Women and Madness by Phyllis Chesler. Copyright (c) 1972 by Phyllis Chesler. Reprinted by permission of Doubleday & Co., Inc. I wish to thank Elizabeth Rosen for informing me of this material.

20. Adapted from "Children's Hour '73: The Zebra Power Story" by Arthur Bell, The Village Voice, March 1, 1973. Copyright (c) 1973 by The Village Voice and reprinted by permission of The Voice and the author.

21. Adapted from "Perspectives on Lesbianism" by Judy Grahn, Women: A Journal of Liberation, Summer, 1970. Copyright (c) 1970 by Women: A Journal of Liberation. Reprinted by permission of Judy Grahn.

22. Adapted from "A Very Difficult Author" by Virgil Thomson, New York Review of Books, Ap. 8, 1971. Copyright (c) 1971 by N.Y. REV Inc. and reprinted by permission. I wish to thank Carole Turbin Miller for informing me of this material.

23. Excerpts from "A Sonatina Followed by Another," Bee Time Vine And Other Pieces by Gertrude Stein, New Haven: Yale Univ. Press, 1953. Copyright (c) 1953 by Alice B. Toklas. Reprinted by permission of Yale University Press.

24. Adapted from a taped interview by Jonathan Katz with one of the Boise victims, Dec. 18, 1973, N.Y.C., and used with his permission.

25. (See note 21 above.)

26. (See note 5 above.)

27. Adapted from the manuscript version of "I Dreamed in a Dream" (Calamus" No. 34 in Leaves of Grass, 1860.)

ACT II

1. Adapted from "Once I Passed Through..." which first appeared as No. 9 of the "Enfans d'Adam" group in the 1860 Leaves of Grass. In all published versions the poem refers to a woman. The manuscript reveals that it originally referred to a male, and it is this version which has been followed.

2. Adapted from Whitman's 1862 diary in the Library of Congress. This diary contains several similar references to street meetings with men whom the poet says he "slept with."

3. Handbuch der Gerlichtlichen Medicin by J.L. Casper and Carl Liman, Berlin: Hirschwald, 1889, Vol. 1. Translation by Jim Steakley.

4. The two informants of Havelock Ellis quoted in Sexual Inversion, Philadelphia: F.A. Davis Co., 1901.

5. Extracted from THE AUTOBIOGRAPHY OF LINCOLN STEEFENS, copyright, 1931, by Harcourt Brace Jovanovich, Inc.; renewed, 1959, by Peter Steffens. Reprinted by permission of the publishers.

6. Adapted from The Female Impersonators by Ralph Werther-Jennie June ("Earl Lind"), ed. by Alfred W. Herzog, N.Y.: The Medico-Legal Journal, 1922.

7. Adapted from 1899 testimony quoted in the N.Y. State Assembly Report of the Special Commission Appointed to Investigate the Public Officials and Police Department of the City of New York, N.Y., 1900. Two witnesses' testimony has been combined. I would like to thank Wilbur Miller for informing me of this document's existence.

8. Adapted from Dancing the Gay Lib Blues by Arthur Bell. Copyright (c) 1971 by Arthur Bell. Reprinted by permission of Simon and Schuster and the author.

9. Excerpted from The American Idea of Success by Richard M. Huber, N.Y.: McGraw-Hill Book Co., 1972. Copyright (c) 1972 by Richard M. Huber. Reprinted by permission of McGraw-Hill and the author. The statement by the Unitarian Church is quoted by Huber and is among the public records of Brewster, Mass.

10. The Weekly Scotsman, 1901, is quoted by Havelock Ellis in Sexual Inversion, Philadelphia; F.A. Davis Co., 1901.

11. Adapted from a story in the Long Island, N.Y., Shelter Island Reporter, Jan. 6, 1973, which quotes from the East Long Island Star, Dec. 31, 1897. I wish to thank Carol and Robert Joyce for informing me of this document.

12. Adapted from material in Studies in the Psychology of Sex, Vol. 2, Sexual Inversion by Havelock Ellis, Philadelphia: 1915.

13. The first two speeches are adapted from "Stepin Fetchit Woman" by Martha Shelley, Come Out!, Nov. 14, 1969. Copyright (c) by Come Out! Reprinted by permission of Martha Shelley. The following speeches are adapted from "The Woman-Identified Woman" written and published by N.Y. Radicalesbians. Copyright (c) 1970 and reprinted by permission of Lois Hart.

14. Ginsberg's testimony is part of the record of the Chicago Conspiracy Trial. Ginsberg's "Love Poem On Theme By Whitman" is in Reality Sandwiches, copyright (c) 1963 by Allan Ginsberg. Reprinted by permission of the author.

15. Adapted from "These Days. Sodom," N.Y. Sun, Nov. 11, 1943.

16. Excerpt from "Time Essay. The Homosexual in America," Time Magazine, Jan. 21, 1966. Reprinted by permission of Time, The Weekly Newsmagazine; Copyright (c) Time Inc.

17. Adapted from Edward the Dyke and Other Poems by Judy Grahn. Copyright (c) 1971 by Judy Grahn. Reprinted by permission of the author and the Women's Press Collective, 5251 Broadway, Oakland, Calif. 94618. I would like to thank Deanna Alida for suggesting this scene.

18. The song "Gay People" is by Deanna Alida and reprinted by her permission. See following.

Production Notes.

Coming Out! is intended to express in theatrical form some of the new feelings and ideas arising out of the recent liberation activities of lesbians and gay men — the sense of justified outrage at our oppression; a new militant determination to subvert the heterosexual dictatorship by organized, united action; a new sense of ourselves as a social group with a history not only of persecution, but also of resistance, not only of difficulty, but also of love; an ability to laugh at the often absurd attitudes of hetero bigots and our own affectations; a new strength and positive sense of ourselves.

This is a political entertainment. It should help gay people focus their anger away from themselves and outward into action against anti-gay institutions. The production should emphasize that, even if our oppression has been internalized by gay people, it ultimately comes from the society outside us. It is also important that, while demonstrating how severe gay oppression has been, all self-pity be avoided; the play should suggest that gays have the alternative of fighting back. Humor and humanity are important; they make the rhetorical speeches digestible. But the serious basis of the humor should not be overlooked; when "camp" humor is used it should always be an expression of defiance directed at our oppressors, not a put-down of ourselves.

Everything possible should be done to set this play specifically within the context of these United States. For example, an upside down American flag, symbolizing a nation in distress — and a gay flag combining interlocked female symbols and interlocked male symbols — might hang above the stage. Although gay persecution exists in other countries, under other systems, it is this country and this system against which our present struggle must be waged. The play gains in impact from its focus on gay life and liberation in this one country.

I originally conceived this play being staged as a rather static "reading." The much more active and dramatic staging suggested here was developed by the original director, David Roggensack, working closely with myself and the original cast over a period of six months. During this work period the lesbians in the cast made an especially important contribution in helping to shape the content and presentation of the women's material in the script.

Our basic theatrical problem, we quickly realized, was to find stage actions which would be dramatic and expressive of, but not necessarily equivalent to those actions described in the narrative. We found that when the action described in words was not explicitly acted out, but left partially to the audience's imagination, it was more emotionally evocative than a literal interpretation. The problem in each episode was to find a theatrical metaphor for the situation described, a metaphor which would clarify and express the narrated events. We felt the metaphorical action should express the events narrated emotionally, intellectually, and dramatically in an economical manner, and without pretentiousness. (Sometimes stage action was played against the literal narraation, as when Stein and Toklas make up a bed and kiss during the speech which denies the sexuality of their relation.) It should be noted that the stage directions contained in this script, and these production notes, are meant only as suggestions. Those stage directions have been included which are needed to indicate a basic production concept for each scene or episode.

Adaptations, additions, and deletions should be made in this script based on current events in the lesbian and gay male movements, the development of gay liberation ideology, changes in American society, the discovery of new material, the location and timing of the particular performance, the abilities of the cast and director, length of rehearsal time, finances, etc. For example, when Coming Out! was performed in 1973 for the embattled gay group on the campus of the University of New Hampshire, the Governor and an influential reactionary newspaper of the State were then joined in a struggle to deny the gay group's funding and existence; the gays, however, were supported by the University administration and students. In this particular performance the most defamatory anti-gay comments of the Governor and his fellow bigots made a dramatic and topical opening for Coming Out! Any script changes should, however, maintain an even balance between female and male material. I would like the play to continue to express an assertive, militant, radical gay liberation philosophy.

Actors should not try to imitate the actual persons they portray, but should strive instead to communicate their own authentic and deepest feelings. All artifice should be avoided in the acting. Everyone in the cast and production should be gay; the shared experience of gayness is the starting point for a creative ensemble. The actors should work from their own gay feelings, and ideas, relating the historical material to their own personal experience, thus making it real for themselves. The fact of gay actors "coming out" and making themselves vulnerable before a live audience is part of this play's demonstrated power. A positive ensemble feeling should be apparent among the cast, in the way the actors relate, touch. Those actors not actually engaged in a specific scene may sit upstage, concentrating upon the ongoing scene. If possible the cast should include at least two Third World people of opposite sexes, and as many different gay life styles and personalities as possible. A "good image" before straight people should not be of concern. Paradoxically, if a production of this play authentically expresses a sense of the gay experience it should become accessible, not only to other gay people, but also to straights.

The "boxes" mentioned in the stage directions were, in the New York production, milk crates painted gray. They were used as seats, and piled upon each other in various fluid arrangements to form steps, platforms, a bed, etc. The clothes worn by the actors should be simple and unpretentious, helping to distinguish and emphasize each actor's individuality. Ten actors, five female and five male, were used in the New York production, although the show could be staged with eight versatile performers; the number of males and females should always be kept even. In order to question "masculine" and "feminine" role-playing men should sometimes play women and women men, but this should not be done when the homosexuality of a particular same-sex relation is important.

Posters or slides of the real persons quoted might be exhibited when these characters are introduced and during their speeches, if the mechanics do not interfere with a smooth presentation or distract. Such pictures might also be made into a photomontage backdrop for the performance. The numbered scene titles may be used as working divisions only, or may be announced by the actors, or appear on placards or slides during the actual production. The speaker's name and date might also appear in written form.

The action should be kept moving from scene to scene without pause, the momentum maintained. The continuity between scenes is often important: an actor playing a certain character in one scene may play a significantly related character in the following scene (e.g. see the transition from the end of The Snake Pit to the start of Horatio Alger). For the sake of drama and excitement the conflicts between characters and points of view should be emphasized, clarified, and made immediate, concrete, and personal.

The structure of the script is not basically chronological. It is arranged in thematic "clusters" (like Whitman's Leaves of Grass) according to content and dramatic qualities. There is, however, some chronological development: material on colonial American sodomy executions is introduced early in the play because it comes early in our history, and serves to establish the length and virulence of gay oppression in this country.

All aspects of the production should be simple, spare, economic, honest, beautiful.

A few helpful principles: Avoid sexism. Avoid racism. Avoid elitism and the "famous gay" syndrone (some famous gays are quoted here because of what they say, not because they're famous.) The personal is political, the political is personal. Although much now divides lesbians and and gay males, and gays of different ages, lifestyles, and values, this play seeks, ecumenically, to emphasize that which unites all gay people against our common oppresor. Gay people of the world unite, you have nothing to lose but your shames!

Alice B. Toklas brownies may be served.

Jonathan Katz,
April, 1975

Music & Words by Deanna Alida

Repeat from beginning to end-full cast singing and clapping.
Repeat with a free, happy expression and improvisational har-
mony. Each new **phrase** growing in volume and intensity. The
last phrase sung with strength and determination.

Reviews for Coming Out!

"The Gay and Narrow Path", "Learn and Live" and "In Straight
America" were reprinted by permission of The Village Voice.
Copyright©by The Village Voice, Inc., 1972.

"Coming Out" by Ian J. Tree and the review by Thane Hampten
were reprinted by permission of Gay Magazine.

"Gay Liberation Play Urges Political Power" by Bruce Husten
was reprinted by permission of The Times Record, Troy, N.Y.

The review which appeared in The Lambda, November, 1972 was
reprinted by permission of the Gay Activists Alliance of
New Jersey.

"On 'Coming Out'" by Nancy Miller was reprinted by permission
of Nancy Miller.

"Off, Off and Away" by Robb Baker was reprinted courtesy of
After Dark Magazine, November, 1972.

The review which appeared in Variety, September 20, 1972, was
reprinted by permission of Variety.

The review which appeared in Where It's At, Vol. 2, No. 11,
Summer 1973, was reprinted by permission of Where It's At.

" Coming Out! at the Night House" was reprinted by permission
of Show Business.

"Gay Life and Liberation Come Alive" was reprinted by permission
of the Rutgers Daily Targum.

"Coming Out--Some Agony, Little Ecstasy" was reprinted by
permission of the West Side Discussion Group.

The review which appeared in the New York Mattachine Times,
July/August, 1972 was reprinted by permission of the Mattachine
Society.

"Theater: On Liberation", "The Gay Life: Cartoon vs. Reality?",
"'Politics is not Art'" and "Furor Over 'The Faggot'" were
reprinted by permission of The New York Times.

"An Intelligent 'Coming Out'" was reprinted by permission of
The Record, Bergen County, N.J.

The review which appeared in Win Magazine, 1973 was reprinted by
permission of Win Magazine.

the village VOICE, *June 22*, 1972

THEATRE

Learn and live

by Dick Brukenfeld

COMING OUT!
A documentary play by Jonathan Katz, directed by David Roggensack, presented by the Gay Activists Alliance at the Firehouse, 99 Wooster Street.

Critics argue that the media has replaced both the novel and theatre in the disseminating of information. Yet the media bears the same relation to what people are thinking as the dictionary does to the living language. It follows public consciousness. Beginning with Epic Theatre and the Living Newspapers, 50 years ago, the stage has dealt with subjects that were either neglected or taboo elsewhere. More recently, Martin Duberman's "In White America" brought theatre audiences a vision of black history long before it became an "in" subject. Al Fann's "King Heroin" hit playgoers in the guts with a picture of a teenager's withdrawl symptoms which could never be as powerful on a television screen, even if the sponsors allowed it. And this season The Latin American Fair of Opinion showed us political persecution south of the border—a subject which inspires our media to look the other way.

Last week the Gay Activists Alliance presented **"COMING OUT,!"** which documents the history of "gay life and liberation in America." We've seen plays about homosexuals, but this is the first show I know of that treats the subject historically. Opening with the June, 1969, Stonewall Resistance against the police when the gay liberation movement went public, "Coming Out!" moves back and forth through American history.

We hear Governor William Bradford and the Reverend John Raynor calling for a clampdown on homosexuality in the colonies in 1642. We hear about Horatio Alger's being accused of having sexual relations with young men in his Massachusetts town in 1866. We get views of Willa Cather living with a young woman in Pittsburgh, and another number introduces us a group of lesbian folk heroes-women who in the early 1900's lived their lives quite thoroughly as men.

Using a kind of story theatre technique, "Coming Out" combines narration and the reciting of quotations from public documents —many, appropriately, from this newspaper—with ensemble performing. It is less a play than a political demonstration, both a rallying point for the gay community and the putting forth of a freshly seen segment of America's history. What holds the show together is the sense that the performers, whether looking into the past or quoting such contemporaries as Merle Miller, David McReynolds, or Allen Ginsberg, are talking about their own lives. I liked "Coming Out's" straightforewardness, and its assertion that people should have the right to determine their own lives. Author Jonathan Katz did a good job of collecting and organizing the information, Judy Grahn contributed a funny sketch about a homosexual woman and her psychiatrist, both writers being acutely aware of public images, and director David Roggensack kept things moving.

* * *

COMING OUT

"I was four years old when I started school. But butch haircut or not, some boys in the third grade took one look at me and said, "Hey, look at the sissy," and they started laughing. It seems to me now that I heard that word at least once five days a week for the next thirteen years, until I skipped town and went to the university. Sissy and all the other words —
pansy,
fairy,
nance,
fruit,
fruitcake,
and less polite epithets. I did not encounter the word faggot until I got to Manhattan. I'll tell you this, though. It's not true, that

saying about sticks and stones; it's words that break your bones."

Merle Miller said it in 1971, and it is one of the more sensitive and moving of a series of published and spoken quotes which forms the base for much of Jonathan Katz' new play at the GAA Firehouse, *Coming Out!*.

Governor William Bradford (1642), Willa Cather, Gertrude Stein, Alice B Toklas, Horatio Alger, Allen Ginsberg, and Walt Whitman figure prominently in the script as do the notorious 1955 Boise fag hunt, the Stonewall Resistance (the 1969 Village riots seem to have taken on the importance of a kind of gay Bastille), The Snake Pit raid (1970) and other incidents encountered on the road to Gay Liberation.

The play, which is related to story, and even street theatre, is well-structured. Katz has expertly interspliced his material and David Roggansack has directed with a lively hand so that it moves smoothly and purposely towards its goal. Goal, not conclusion or climax (unless one considers the energetic applause and cheers of the audience a climax), because *Coming Out!* seems more concerned with proselytizing than with drama per se.

"Out of the closets and into the streets," "Lesbians unite — I am your worst fear and greatest fantasy" and "Until we have power — we'll never be free" are examples of the kind of propaganda that often crops up in the work. I suspect it was designed to raise the consciousness of the overwhelmingly gay crowds who attended the SRO performances, and if so, it succeeds admirably. They cheered and bravoed and hissed and sighed and moaned and remained so absolutely quiet and attentive that it became apparent that Jonathon Katz knew what the hell he was talking about. If catharsis is what theatre is all about, then *Coming Out!* is a textbook example, provided the audience is gay. Heterosexuals, however, for whom the question of Gay Liberation is not as immediate an issue, may be expected to view the work in somewhat different terms.

Merle Miller's lyricism is touching, the Chicago Conspir-

acy Trial provocative, "The Psychoanalysis of Edward the Dyke" uproariously funny and the play generally informative. But the work's greatest weakness, its recurring propaganda keeps gnawing away at the periphery of our rapport. I think a gay audience would tend to ignore or else revel in this proselytizing approach, but heterosexuals will probably be at first irritated and later distracted. It's somewhat similar to the harangue-like atmosphere at racial equality, women's lib and anti-war rallies. We enjoy the entertainment, and are properly enlightened by new developments or unique views. But look, we're all good leftist-liberals; we're already for equality and against the war, so why doesn't somebody stop trying so desperately to convince us? Maybe because there are a few in the audience who need to be converted and a few more whose faith needs to be reaffirmed, in which case it becomes somewhat excusable at a rally.

The main problem with *Coming Out!* seems to be that the show is situated midway between political rally and theatre. As the former, it is an unmitigated success; as the latter, somewhat less so.

One of the show's greatest assets is the honesty of its author and the shiny-faced earnestness of its actors. The issues presented are emotional and crucial, yet on the night I attended, there was a certain innocence and optimism present, not just on the stage where all cynicism-producing slickness has been foregone, but among the audience as well. The play demonstrates and the audience reinforced the impression that in their search for political and social liberation homosexuals have already achieved a certain personal freedom. It doesn't matter who it is, one senses and immediately respects somebody who is honest with himself.

From the play, Merle Miller:

"When I was a child in Marshalltown, Iowa, I hated Christmas, but loved Halloween. I never wanted to take off the mask; I wanted to wear it everywhere, night and day, always. It took me almost

fifty years to come out of the closet, to stop pretending to be something I was not."

— Robert Pierce

Off Broadway...

BY IAN J. TREE

COMING OUT

Well, I really hope that everyone has been fortunate enough to see the documentary play *Coming Out*, presented by the Arts Committee of the Gay Activists Alliance —written by Jonathan Katz and directed by David Roggensack.

There were two "acts" and as the footnote mentioned in the program, the play, is "adapted from fiction, poetry, autobiographical and historical accounts."

I must admit I was surprised by the excellence of the entire production on all levels. David Roggensack's direction was professional and the additional dialogue and script by Jonathan Katz was well written and very pointed in several places, enough to bring great cheers and knowing smiles from the highly partisan crowd.

"Act 1" began appropriately enough with the Stonewall Resistance on June 27-29, 1969—and with that the beginning of the Gay Liberation Movement as we know it today. The play continued with utterances by Merle Miller, Kate Millet, Sue Katz, radicalesbians, and Marty Robinson—all about *coming out*. Further words by Merle Miller and Spiro Agnew, including the famous, or rather infamous "effete snobs." It treated of famous love affairs—Willa Cather and Isabelle McClung in the early twentieth century; Gertrude Stein and Alice B. Toklas. Quotations from "Hands" by Sherwood Anderson in 1911. The Witch Hunt, Boise, Idaho, 1955 (read John Gerassi's *The Boys of Boise*. It reads like a modern Salem witch hunt.). Exchanges between Seymour Krim and David McReynolds of the *Village Voice*, in 1955 and again between Virgil Thompson and Patricia Meyerwitz in 1971.

The "second act" included recitations from Walt Whitman's "City of Orgies," the Horatio Alger affair in 1866; The Snake Pit raid in March, 1970; Lesbian Folk Heroes of the early 1900's; the Diego Vignales affair in 1970 which was part of the Snake Pit raid. The young man was from Argentina, I believe, and was so frightened by the raid and subsequent arrest that he jumped from a second-story window of the police department only to impale himself on the iron fence below. It continued with Allen Ginsberg and the Chicago Conspiracy Trial of 1969, wherein he recited one of his poems based on one by Walt Whitman—a modern version which I cannot believe did not color the ears of the court.

The play ended with "The Psychoanalysis of Edward the Dyke" by Judy Grahn, and in my own "umble" opinion, it was the highpoint of the evening. It was extremely funny and marvelously acted by Steve Krotz as the psychoanalyst and Deanna Alida as Edward the Dyke. The play ended with a section from John Osborn's *The Entertainer*, and finally the first Gay-in.

Blake Bergrren, Charlie Brown, Bruce Buchy, Deanna Alida, Helen Sandra Weinberg and Steve Krotz were outstanding in their respective "roles." I think every few of the performers had had any real previous acting experience, but most of them, nevertheless, seem to have a good sense of the timing required for "feeling" their lines and making them believable. The others were not as comfortable with their lines, especially the poetry recitations which require a finely honed sense of that same timing and "feeling."

I must congratulate David Roggensack on his direction and I feel that he really succeeded in bringing together both parts of the Gay Lib Movement; i.e., the boys and the girls. I talked with him afterwards about the possibility of putting on a limited-run on off-Broadway. They had thought about it, he said, but if it were to happen, they would want "gay money" (i.e., a gay sponsor and genuine interest in what the play has to offer). At any rate, he said he would keep us informed.

For those of you lucky enough to see it, I'm sure you would agree that the next logical step *is* an off-Broadway run. It's really an excellent production and with a little more room to breathe and stretch its legs, it could go a long way in not only bringing out extreme closet cases, but always setting the "straight" community straight on the bad-mouthing and bad press homosexuals have so long received and how Gay Liberation has begun to change all of that. Like my friend Daniel once said—"somebody *do* something."

NEW YORK MATTACHINE TIMES,
JULY/AUG 1972

COMING OUT! a play by Jonathan Katz

During Gay Pride Week, the Arts Committee of GAA, New York, put on a work-
shop production of a play by Jonathan Katz
called COMING OUT. I would have subtitled it "A Dialogue for Chorus" but for
the pure propaganda output about the Gay
movement starting from comments and works
written from 1642 on, the work was sheer
joy.

What Mr. Katz has done is take passages
from fiction, poetry, autobiographical
and historical accounts from such people
as Willa Carter, Alexander Berkman, Allen
Ginsberg, Gertrude Stein, etc., and put
their words to movement and dramatization.
As wonderful as the quotes were, I found
Mr. Katz's own words, used for many of the
skits, much more to today's action.

The cast was too large to list them all,
but each and every one gave their all to
a project that is dear to all of us. The
direction by David Roggensack was excellent. There has been talk of getting the
production Off-Broadway, but there is a
hugh amount of copywrite clearance to
obtain. I myself would like to see the
production opened to the public. Maybe,
just maybe, it might help them to understand the movement in terms of human
people instead of just headlines. For the
Firehouse, maybe ten minutes could have
been cut from each act (there are two acts),
but for Off-Broadway it could be expanded
into three sharp, fast-paced, fast moving,
hit them where it hurts, acts. Time will
tell. For those of you fortunate enough to
have seen it, you know what I'm talking
about. For those that missed it, well,
you missed one of the highlights of Gay
Pride Week '72.

marc williams

BY THANE HAMPTEN

I haven't had the opportunity yet to recommend to you the Jonathan Katz documentary play, *Coming Out*, I saw it during Gay Pride Week at Gay Activists Alliance Firehouse. I went expecting a tedious, humorless, amateurish exercise in agitprop that would have all the subtlety and artistry of a Bulgarian knife-throwing act. Imagine my surprise when it turned out to be a funny, intensely moving and beautiful experience.

The play is long and throws mind-boggling tons of data at you. I was sitting on the dirty floor, in the aisle, in a ridiculously contorted position. My legs were numb and I was almost trampled three times by the exiting players. We were not allowed to smoke. It was hot. Many lesser impositions upon my sensitive nature have caused me to flee theatres during intermission, if not sooner. However, I *gladly* stuck it out and was sorry when the play ended.

If ever there was a penultimate definition of the meaning of Gay Pride, and an illuminating celebration in homage of that spirit, it is *Coming Out*. It also benefited from the excitingly fast-paced and inventive direction of David Roggensack,

and the enthusiastic and amazingly professional attitude of the performers. (And what incredible memories they have!)

I found it difficult to believe that this vital and often inspirational work would be allowed to languish and die. I hardly expected Norman Jewison to film it for United Artists release, yet I felt that it surely deserved more exposure than the hospitable but limited run at The Firehouse.

Now I'm pleased to report that according to GAA press representative, the everhelpful Charles Choset, there are plans to seek production off-Broadway and on college campuses.

Best and most positive of all, *Coming Out* will be given in a series of performances, September 7 though 17, at the Washington Square United Methodist Church (113 West 4th St.). I'd like to encourage you to treat yourself to this delightful and pertinent celebration. (By the way, did you know that one of Roget's synonyms for *celebration* are the words "coming out"? How accurate!) If you don't leave the theatre a better and happier person, you're *dead*, baby.

An intelligent 'Coming Out'

By EMORY LEWIS
Drama Critic

On the broadway stage, homosexuals and lesbians have always been the butt of crude and cruel jokes, usually in walk-on roles in comedies. However, the gay liberation movement is determined to change that image.

LEWIS

The theater wing of the Gay Activists Alliance plans a series of plays you won't find on Broadway. Last night, the politically-minded Alliance opened a new play, "Coming Out!," at the Washington Square Methodist Church, which has been home to Leroi Jones' searing "Slave Ship," the brilliant Grotowski troupe from Poland, and several productions of the seminal Open Theater.

"Coming Out!" is subtitled "a documentary play about gay life and liberation in America" and is culled from fiction, poetry, autobiography, and historical records. It was created by new playwright Johathan Katz, and it has been superbly staged by David Roggensack, who is otherwise occupied as a theater pubilicity agent.

"I found "Coming Out!" informative, sensitive, and engrossing. There are weak moments when its propaganda seems too obvious or too strident, but in general it is a most intelligent theater-piece on an extremely controversial subject.

Became politicized

The evening opens with the Stonewall resistance in June of 1969, when gay boys and girls fought the police who tried to close their favorite Greenwich Village bar. This was the beginning, the text implies, of the politicalization of gay persons in America. Since that time, homosexuals have formed political organizations all over the U.S.

The skits cover American gay history from the hysterical witch-hunts of the Puritans in 1642 through the mass Gay-Ins in Central Park in the 1970's. There is a fascinating and illuminating segment on the lesbian affair between novelist Willa Cather and a Pittsburgh heiress. Gertrude Stein, Walt Whitman, Merle Miller, and Allen Ginsberg are quoted in detail in several sketches. There is an informative segment on the trial of Horatio Alger on charges of homosexuality.

Some of the language is raw. There is a certain amount of kissing and fondling by members of the same sex. If you are easily offended by this, I suggest you do not go.

Awful to superlative

The cast consists of five boys (Bruce Buchy, Robert Heine, Charlie Brown, Michael Lee, and Jim Robiscoe) and five girls (Deanna Alida, Carolyn Nowodzinski, Elizabeth Rosen, Helen Sandra Weinberg, and Emily Rubin Weiner).

They are all dressed in blue jeans, and they range in talent from awful to superlative.

The best of the performers is Deanna Alida, who is an opera singer with a extraordinary vocal range. In the funniest skit of the evening, she impersonates a lady in psychoanalysis who is trying to lose her interest in girls. It's a devastating attack on conventional Freudian analysis, and Miss Alida is a first-rate comic.

Incidentally, "Coming Out," after its off-Broadway run, will tour the East. As of this writing, it is scheduled to play Paramus in mid-October, under the auspices of the Gay Activists Alliance of New Jersey. The theater has not yet been set.

the village VOICE, *September* 14, 1972

THEATRE

In straight America

by Michael Feingold

A play is a creation that offers all kinds of possibilities; a documentary play, however, really offers only one, which I think might best be called "certification." Whether it's organized towards one climactic event, like Kipphardt's "J. Robert Oppenheimer," or a looser historical survey, like Duberman's "In White America," what the documentary offers us is the opportunity to come into emotional contact with facts. Facts we already knew are made more vivid by forcing us to focus so centrally on them; facts we didn't know are driven home with more dramatic (naturally) emphasis than they have if we merely run across them in a book. The theatre, the placing of the facts in that arena, to be judged by the audience, stamps them with importance. So if you think gay liberation is important (and I expect even its opponents would agree the movement is a significant phenomenon), "**COMING OUT!**", Jonathan Katz's documentary play on the subject, is a useful thing to have around, and probably the best project the Arts Committee of the Gay Activists Alliance, its producers, could conceive. The pattern of the work, though not chronological, is otherwise that of "In White America" and similar creations, excerpts from news reports, speeches, historical commentary, and documents, interspersed with first person reminiscences, excerpts from relevant works of fiction, and so forth. "In White America" started with the slave ships and ended with the desegregation of Little Rock's Central High School. The more militant "Coming Out" begins with the Stonewall Resistance and the formation of the Gay Lib movement, flashes back to Governor Bradford's 1642 proclamation against sodomy, and moves on, rather randomly, to the compiler's own account of the first annual Gay-In . Some of the material is to be expected: Whitman, Gertrude Stein, Allen Ginsberg, Sherwood Anderson's "Hands." Other parts—a French tourist's account of Philadelphia Lesbians in 1793; the romance of Willa Cather and Isabelle McClung; police raids on New York gay bars in 1899—are pleasant surprises. The material is infallibly interesting, and Mr. Katz and David Roggensack, his director, have made an effective and informing evening of it, which ought to pique the interest of straight audiences, as well as inspiring healthy feelings of political openness in gay ones.

The cast, for some odd reason, is entirely amateur—odd because there are certainly enough gay professional actors in New York to staff a project of this sort. Nor am I convinced that only gay actors ought to be used, any more than I thought Joseph Papp needed to cast his abortive stage version of "Winning Hearts and Minds" solely with Vietnam veterans. Authenticity onstage has to do with how well you protect the words, actions, and feelings, not with whether you really own them offstage. As it is, I lost some interesting passages in "Coming Out," and don't feel the cast gets nearly as much out of the texts as a trained one might; their evident devotion, however, has inspired them all to a dignity that is the mark of the best amateur work, and is at times extremely moving.

* * *

Off-Broadway Review

Coming Out

The Arts Committee of the Gay Activists Alliance presentation of a documentary play in two acts by Jonathan Katz. Staged by David Roggensack; lighting, Dempster Leach Enterprises; technical director, Bud Pitman; production stage manager, Reed Lenti; publicity, Howard Atlee. Opened Sept. 7, '72, at the Washington Square Methodist Church, N.Y.; all seats $2.

Cast: Deanna Alida, Charlie Brown, Bruce Buchy, Robert Heine, Michael Lee, Carolyn Nowodzinski, Jim Robiscoe, Elizabeth Rosen, Carolyn Nowodzinski, Jim Robiscoe, Elizabeth Rosen, Helen Sandra Weinberg, Emily Rubin Weiner.

Overt agitation - propaganda plays are usually poor risks as theatre and this one about the emergence of homosexuality from the closet unfortunately tends to support the rule. While there are rewarding moments in this two-act documentary — perhaps thrilling for the convinced — the Jonathan Katz work is too long, and too static.

The production, sponsored by the Arts Committee of the Gay Activists Alliance, may have potential for productions at non-other GAA chapters and might fare reasonably well on the college circuit. The b.o. prospects seem severly limited, mostly because of lackluster quality rather than subject matter.

Katz has assembled 22 scenes based on various historical and contemporary documents, reports, poetic and autobiographical accounts, trial hearings and news clippings. The play begins with a recreation of the vigorous resistance to a police raid on a Greenwich Village gay bar.

That was virtually the first time gay people banded together to fight what they charged was obvious oppression. The 22-scene collage ends with a banal and somewhat surprising "When the Gays Go Marching In."

In between are sandwiched some interesting historical bits — via examination of novelist Willa Cather's lesbian relationship, investigations of N.Y. police around the turn of the century, a homosexual witch hunt in Boise in 1955 — and seemingly interminable quotations from Walt Whitman, most badly delivered.

The cast is obviously unprofessional but indicates conviction and a contagious intensity. David Roggensack's staging is clever in most scenes, he moves actors about with invention, but lacks dramatic punch. The firstnite audience, apparently pre-committed to the cause, seemed less responsive than might have been expected.

Overall, "Coming Out" seems safe enough for situations pretested for favorability. In choppier commercial seas, the show could well sink under the weight of its own verbiage.   *Sege.*

The gay and narrow path

by Michael Feingold

Eduardo Corbe's "THE BITCHES," at Theatre of the Americas. has reminded me very emphatically of something I had no space to take up last week when I discussed the GAA's production of "Coming Out!" the quality of homosexual life in this country (if you'll pardon my adapting that overused phrase) and the extent to which "Coming Out!" does *not* reflect it, being in fact more of a dream of what gay society might be than a thorough depiction of its actuality.

I don't mean these remarks as a negative criticism of "Coming Out!" A group committed to the political and social liberation of homosexuals, as GAA is, has an obligation to present that ideal image of gay behavior to the world. But in dreams, as Yeats said, begins responsibility, and GAA and its sibling groups have likewise an obligation to face the realities of homosexual life—constricted, squalid, neurotic-compulsive as it so often is—and think about reforming it from within, i. e., socially, as well as from without, in terms of the legal barriers and larger social stigmas the group is so usefully laboring to destroy.

One passage in "Coming Out!" troubled me in particular: the replay of a late—'50's debate carried on in this newspaper between Seymour Krim and David McReynolds. Krim foresaw the emergence of the gay minority as a political force; McReynolds denied the possibility of same. The show's treatment of McReynolds is understandably bitter: his words are rather rudely burlesqued, which annoyed me because they seemed full of perceptive comments on such matters as the coldness or false sentimentality of certain forms of homosexual art; the mechanical, obsessive nature of cruising and other aspects of gay sex relations; the crushing emptiness of lives with no serious concerns other than that of simultaneously hiding and signalling their sexual orientation. Why should an intelligent gay spokesman like McReynolds be so roughhandled for pointing out facts? (Especially when his own confession of homosexuality, in an earlier part of the show, is presented with virtual reverence.) It seems to me his only error was in not predicting that all this repression could lead only to an explosion; unfortunately a wise man is not always qualified to be a tipster.

That McReynolds's criticism of homosexual life still holds true is borne out, as I started to say a few paragraphs ago, by "The Bitches," which is, quite literally, an all-male version of "The Women," blow by heart-rending blow, with the unseen adulterer in a gay marriage dissected by a chorus of gay gossips romping shrilly from baths to boutique to Fire Island bar. As with Mrs. Luce's original, the play is festeringly hypocritical: after letting its audience wallow in the pleasures of bitchery for 10 plodding scenes, the obligatory Gay Lib happy ending is nailed on with some tears-of-joy nonsense about the now-reunited couple driving bitchery and unmanliness out of their lives and standing up before the world as what they are—"two men who happen to like each other." One's only response is a desperate desire to bash the author-director and everyone else involved over the head with lambda-shaped cudgels. The whole thing is staged and performed with a heavy-handed archness that would make John Gilbert and Norma Shearer look askance; the mostly-male audience seemed to adore every excruciating second.

I don't know what attitude, if any, GAA takes officially about such phenomena as this and the other trashy gay plays that are taking unfair advantage of the new openness the liberation movement has stimulated. I suspect some discussion of the subject might be useful. At any rate I think it unfair, under the circumstances, to belittle someone who is able to observe the situation, and describe it as honestly as David McReynolds.

* * *

Our man on the Aisle

the WestSider

OCT., 1972 Vol.2 NO. 11

A SPECIAL REVIEW by Jack Reid
"COMING OUT" — Some Agony, Little Ecstasy

"COMING OUT" – a play by Jonathan Katz, directed by David Roggensack, lately at Washington Square Methodist Church; now scheduled at various other locations and for various playdates.

As a member of the jaded generation (i.e., by today's standards - anyone older than 23), I felt there wasn't much about Gay Life that I didn't know about. I was wrong. *"Coming Out"* informed me; taught me; raised my consciousness.

Billed as a documentary, *Coming Out* is less a play than a history lesson of what it means to be Gay. A 22-piece pastiche of prose, poetry, narrative, and exposition, the two-hour show is gutsy and well-written. The material is fast-paced and should grip one's attention to the end.

Some people may feel that *Coming Out* is too polemical — that we are being handed propaganda instead of entertainment. Perhaps this *is* so, but the message that the author is giving us is so vital, I question whether if presented in another way it would be as effective. Granted, to some the message will be messy; some people *will* squirm. Good! It draws an accurate bead on bigotry. It should make everyone a bit more aware of how things really are. Awareness may be only the first step in a long journey, but

it is an *indispensible* step, and should have been taken sooner.

There are parts that are overdone, e.g., the radical lesbian bit. Perhaps the shrill and strident shrieks may win some women to their cause, but I wonder how many allies will be alienated in the meantime. I grant them the right to make their point — but must they stab me with it?

There is one skit that is delightful — "The Psychoanalysis of Edward the Dyke." It reiterates with subtlety and delicious humor the same points made throughout the evening, but with such a difference! The truths sneak up on you instead of bludgeoning you head on.

Though staging is minimal -- just a few (appropriate) soap boxes -- the acting is good. The cast is young and spirited and works very hard. The only thing that would tip off the audience that they are amateurs is their delivery. Perhaps the director can help them project better, enunciate more clearly, and speak more slowly. They certainly have the right feeling and attitude for the material.

This is a play that is good for the collective group consciousness. It is not a frivolous work. This is a play that should benefit both straight and gay alike. I hope it will be around and available so that more will be able to see it. We think you'll find it a worthwhile evening.

.........Jack Reid

Gay life and liberation come alive

By Lorraine Grassano

"Coming Out" is not a *story about* gay life and liberation in the USA, it *is* gay life and liberation come alive — come full alive — free from guilt and fear. Jonathan Kat's documentary is the first play to be born out of the gay liberation movement. All the thirteen people involved in the production are gay and proud to be gay. The five men and women who act do not wear masks. It is their own thoughts, experiences, and inner conflicts that they relive while re-enacting the lives of the gay and anti-gay historical figures. In the last scene the historical date is 1972 and now; thus the stage is completely disolved and the actors play no parts at all: they are themselves and they invite the audience to talk with them.

Gay Liberation has two fronts: the law and the self. Appropriately, then, in the first act of "Coming Out", the emphasis is on gays as an oppressed minority group, and in the second act, on gays as deviants. The scenes "With Hunt, Boise, Idaho, 1955" and "Hands" are shocking examples of the persecution that has been directed against gays. But tragedy is contrasted with rebellion in this first act. The gays demand their rights as individuals while crying out for unity: "Until we have the power, we'll never be free!"

However, legal freedom is only half the battle. In the second act, gays are labeled as perverted and abnormal and unnatural, and throughout much of gay history, they have believed and accepted this status. Walt Whitman, in the scene "City of Orgies", comes to the defense not only of gays but of all "so-called" perverts. The battle then becomes one of Puritanism versus Pleasure.

Thus Jonathan Katz gives to gayness a universal significance. He presents homosexuality as part of the struggle for human rights and human happiness — a struggle which all men grapple with in some form. That is why straight people can also identify with the characters in "Coming Out".

Anyone who saw "The Boys in the Band" must see "Coming Out". The pitiful, self-tormented homosexual is just one part o the gay mind and the gay history — a part which is beginning to break free. Jonathan Kats says of his play: "It is the beginning of a new culture."

Women loving women

Women, especially, must see "Coming Out." Just as the women actors protest on stage against a male-orientated society, so they protested behind stage in order to change the script which was originally male dominated. Deanna Alida, one of the women actors, stated, "The script was set and we unset it. Each of us five women worked to bring out the female point of view more equally."

Here then is another example of the thin line between the act and the actual which gives "Coming Out" its power. When they had finished, the female view actually dominated. The second act, which is the more impressionable of thy two, is overwhelmingly women-orientated. The scene "Lesbian Folk Heroes" pantomimes the lives of women who posed as men to escape the drudgery of early 19th-century female roles. One need not be a lesbian to cheer heartily during this amusing scene. "The Psychoanalysis of Edward the Dyke" will have everyone in histerics. In this episode, a lesbian is cured of her perversion thusly: after she is shown the body of a naked female, she is given a horrible electric shock; then she is shown a sugar-coated penis and the doctor gives her a lollypop. In a more serious scene, lesbianism is defined as "the rage of all women condensed to the point of explosion." At the end of the play, the ultimate statement concerning women's liberation is spoken: "We used to love a woman to be like a man. Now we are *women* loving women."

Both the men and women actors, at the end of "Coming Out," shout out slogans to demonstrate that they are breaking free—that "The masks are coming off." The drama mask of tragedy is replaced by a face of anger and rebellion; the mask of comedy is replaced by a face of rejoicing—no longer will gays allow themselves to be the object of mocking. or the mockers.

"Coming Out" will make its college debut here at Rutgers, Monday at 8 p.m. in the Multi-Purpose room of RSC. I do hope all students will come, take off their own masks and listen to what is being said. The play is an informative history, a thought-provoking bibliography, an explosive psychology. "Coming Out" is the revolution of a group, and, more important, it is the evolution of the individual: from self-oppression to self-expression.

Central Jersey Gay Activists Alliance,
The Lambda,
Nov., 1972

Coming Out! ...the very name promises a show to be remembered. For those of us who have come out, the title evokes memories of our first struggles...for those who were(and are)active in the movement, it brought back scenes of past and present triumphs. "Coming Out" is a play of triumphs. Yes, it is a play of defeats, too. It is a song of life...of gay life. It is a memory of things past, a view of things present, a promise of things yet to be. It is a drama, a comedy, a satire. It is beautiful, it is ugly, it is common, it is rare. It brought many to the point of tears, both from sadness and from laughter. It reminded us that we are not alone in our struggle, nor are we a small group huddled in the darkness. It reminded us that there are friends in the night and it warned us that there are evils not yet dead in the world. It told us once again that we are proud (as if we need to be told) and showed us what we had to be proud of. It prodded those who have become settled and inactive that there are many battles yet to be fought and it summoned back memories of battles that were fought for us.

It was an unbelievable evening. If you are gay, and haven't seen "Coming Out," you must see it. It is a requirement for every person... for those gay and for those straight. It is beautiful, sad, thought provoking. It is one of the most together experiences I have had in many a year. I cannot find the adjectives to describe what I felt during that evening; nor will I try to use those at hand for they would cheapen the experience.

Let me say that "Coming Out" is a masterpiece and that is an understatement. Let me say that the people who acted in it were superb, and let let that be an understatement, too. Let me say thank you on behalf of every gay to the author for his research and to the director for his insight and power of direction. And let me say a separate thank you to GAANJ for bringing this experience to me and my gay sisters and brothers. Bravo!

Coming Out! ...the very name promises a show to be remembered. For those of us who have come out, the title evokes memories of our first struggles...for those who were(and are)active in the movement, it brought back scenes of past and present triumphs. "Coming Out" is a play of triumphs. Yes, it is a play of defeats, too. It is a song of life...of gay life. It is a memory of things past, a view of things present, a promise of things yet to be. It is a drama, a comedy, a satire. It is beautiful, it is ugly, it is common, it is rare. It brought many to the point of tears, both from sadness and from laughter. It reminded us that we are not alone in our struggle, nor are we a small group huddled in the darkness. It reminded us that there are friends in the night and it warned us that there are evils not yet dead in the world. It told us once again that we are proud (as if we need to be told) and showed us what we had to be proud of. It prodded those who have become settled and inactive that there are many battles yet to be fought and it summoned back memories of battles that were fought for us.

It was an unbelievable evening. If you are gay, and haven't seen "Coming Out," you must see it. It is a requirement for every person... for those gay and for those straight. It is beautiful, sad, thought provoking. It is one of the most together experiences I have had in many a year. I cannot find the adjectives to describe what I felt during that evening; nor will I try to use those at hand for they would cheapen the experience.

Let me say that "Coming Out" is a masterpiece and that is an understatement. Let me say that the people who acted in it were superb, and let let that be an understatement, too. Let me say thank you on behalf of every gay to the author for his

research and to the director for his insight and power of direction. And let me say a separate thank you to GAANJ for bringing this experience to me and my gay sisters and brothers. Bravo!

FLASH----Ed Baily here, at the GAANJ sensitivity session. WAY OUT!! I have been in many therapy sessions, both sensitivity and ration, and this was one of the most unbelievable yet. Wild, and well handled. Tony did a beautiful job of guiding us through the hidden inhibitions of our minds. Keep up the good work GAANJ it is easy to see why you are the leading group in New Jersey. New ideas and new techniques should be a definite part of the Gay Movement---- RIGHT ON!!!!!!!!

---

the air
the earth
the stars
the trees
and the universe
are free,
so why aren't us?

AFTER DARK   November 1972
Off, Off and Away
by Robb Baker

Moving on: Fall has brought with it a whole new crew of gay theater entries to the OOB scene. I feel, in general, that gay theater (like black theater or any other theater) should be judged by the same standards as any theater in the same financial league (an OOB gay play should be as good as any other OOB play in terms of production, directing, acting, etc., and shouldn't get biased treatment, pro or con); but this also means that gay theater should be open to a whole range of styles and themes, just as theater-in-general is.

This season's gay offerings present just such a gamut in subject matter (a political documentary, an occult melodrama, a "serious" play, and a screaming comedy), but unfortunately the range in quality is broad as well. On the minus side are *Bluebird* (one of those closet-queen, voyeuristic pieces of crap with one of those "indefinite" preview runs, it is the perfect successor to the pretentious garbage which preceded it at the Mercer Shaw, *And They Put Handcuffs on the Flowers*) and *I Have Always Believed in Ghosts* (an amateurish production at the New Old Reliable, its only selling point being Craig Dudley running around in and out of a whole wardrobe of tank-tops). On the other hand, there was *Coming Out!*, a dramatic collage of newspaper articles, historical documents, poetry and prose dealing with gay liberation, presented at Washington Square Methodist Church. The script, by Jonathan Katz, is outstanding (and should be published post haste), and the support it received from director David Roggensack and the ten young actors involved was superb. Carefully avoiding the pitfalls of preachiness and self-pity (though Merle Miller was quoted a little more kindly than he deserves), the production was a vitally human, extremely moving experience. Gay Activists Alliance groups around the country now plan to mount their own versions, which should boost a good cause considerably.

GAA politicos, however, were no doubt appalled at *The Bitches*, which played three weeks at the New York Theatre of the Americas in anticipation of a general opening later this fall. It is (as GAA would say) swishy, campy, draggy—all those nasty "self-oppressive" things so "destructive to the homosexual life style." Exactly. It's also hysterical, funny, real, down-to-earth—and sexy. Unlike *Boys in the Band*, this is gay humor for a gay audience, not suburban housewives out for a giggle. People who are human enough to laugh at themselves have always interested me a lot more then poker-faced radicals or soul-searching academics anyway. *The Bitches* is the perfect flip side of coin to *Coming Out!* and deserves to run forever, with its no-holds-barred one-liners,

Theater: On Liberation

'Coming Out!' and a Maoist Play Make Rewarding Twin Bill at Night House

By HOWARD THOMPSON

A tiny, Off Broadway show-case called the Night House (at 249 West 18th Street) is playing a novel, rewarding double bill linked with a lib-eration theme.

The first half of the bill seen last Saturday was a two-hour work about homosexual-ity, titled "Coming Out!" Ten young men and women in denims and sports shirts cheerfully bounced into the tiny auditorium and proudly advocated homosexual free-dom. Their sharp, supple pan-tomiming ranged from funny to heartrending. The con-tent, quoting newspapers, diaries, essays and such au-thors as Sherwood Anderson, Gertrude Stein, Willa Cather and Merle Miller, was imagi-natively compiled by Jonathan Katz and directed accordingly by David Roggensack. The format is similar to Martin Dubeman's "In White Amer-ica."

The cast, especially Deanna Alida, Elizabeth Rosen, Michael O'Connor and Charlie Brown, could not have been more effective.

•

For the second play the bare stage floor was trans-formed by bright colors. To tinkling music, we see the in-terior of a Chinese village home, dominated, by a large picture of Mao Tse-tung. What follows is an English adaptation (by the co-produ-cer, David Gaard) of Sun Yu's prize-winning play, "The Women's Representative," heralding the rising role of women (in 1953) in the Peo-ple's Republic of China.

Paying dutiful tribute to the Chinese Government the 75-minute play is, essenti-ally, a simple five-character exercise, stressing spunk— that of a rebellious wife tied to an old-fashioned family. As this "Doll's House" hero-ine, Linda Kampley is abso-lutely darling. Good, too, are Dolores Kenan, Lisa Shreve and Roberta Pikser. The one jarring note is Dempster Leech's broad portrayal of the husband.

Timothy Miles did the at-tractive set and costumes. Pamela De Sio has directed with charm an exotic novelty whose quietly persuasive theme and basic values could apply anywhere.

It plays alone Wednesday, then is bracketed with "Com-ing Out!" Friday through Sunday. For reservations, call 691-7359.

SHOW BUSINESS

COMING OUT!

at the Night House — by **DEBBI WASSERMAN**

Tired of being a closet culture, the gay society is coming out, demanding respect and insisting on being recognized. To this end, author Jonathan Katz has excellently researched and assembled material from the history and literature of homosexuals. Then, under the capable direction of David Roggensack, assisted by ten sensitive actors (both male and female), the case is definitively stated. Important points are made, are clarified, and are re-made; and although the result is often unnecessary repetition, COMING OUT remains interesting, is always theatrically valid, and proves to be effective.

Mr. Roggensack's production is designed to highlight the various concepts of the play. To emphasize the underlying theme of strength through unity, the actors continually group together, with their arms intertwined, as they watch each other plead their case. Then, from this basic physical structure, they create meaningful aesthetic tableaux, or ably perform pantomimes to further clarify what is being said and to add life to a series of potentially didactic lectures. Through their self-respectful manner, the precise staging, and an over-all sense of humor, they demonstrate that homosexuality is more than a way of having sex — it is a way of life, and of love as well. In this way, they not only show but say, that they, too, have a right to be accepted as part of today's society.

In many ways, COMING OUT is idealistic in its portrayal of homosexual life and thought, and one-sided in its condemnation of society as the sole cause of their troubles. Yet, at the same time, through logic, poetry and documentation, Mr. Katz makes many poignant and pertinent points — not only about homosexual prejudice, but also about its effect on racism and anti-feminism. The play deserves to be heard, and this production makes it enjoyable to listen to.

So forget about the desperation and sadness of THE FAGGOT, and get thee to the Night House, 249 W. 18th Street, to see COMING OUT!, a joyous, proud experience. COMING OUT! is an interpretive documentary play about gay liberation in the U.S., written and assembled by Jonathan Katz, directed with great dexterity by David Roggensack, and acted by an articulate, bright, all-gay cast of five men and five women. COMING OUT! touches all the bases that THE FAGGOT does, but in a sympathetic, realistic and current manner, presenting the many sides of many-sided gay life and lore and then saying, "Decide for yourself what you feel about all of this." Well, right on, COMING OUT! There is militancy here, but not too much. There is political thought here, but not too much. The idea, among others, that gays are human beings first, and homosexuals secondarily, is presented here, and this is a thought that I've always subscribed to, but not one that YOU need necessarily believe - and the actors tell you this. For the first time in the theatre, I felt that I was being treated to various gay ideas as a gay being with enough of a mind to choose what I care to agree with and what I don't care to buy. What a joy! Gay is coming of age theatrically.

THE FAGGOT has been using a quote from Newsday in its advertising: "The most insightful, unsentimental and entertaining examination of this particular touchy subject ever to occupy a New York stage." It's a good quote - but for COMING OUT! COMING OUT! never preaches or sentimentalizes, but it is consistantly interesting and entertaining. Beginning with the Stonewall riot in 1969, and ending at last year's gay march, the work includes historical and fictional writings of Willa Cather, Gertrude Stein (a much more pleasant lady here than in THE FAGGOT), Christopher Isherwood, Sherwood Anderson (his staggering story, "Hands," brilliantly closes the first act), Walt Whitman, Allen Ginsberg, and many others, and the sexual emphasis is divided equally between gay men and women. In fact, COMING OUT! breaks new theatrical ground in that it's the first show where guys play girls, whites play blacks, and so on, but only when the ensemble-style of the show demands it; in other words, this is not used as a device or as a truck, but merely as a way to illuminate certain material. Writing this, the method sounds pretentious and offensive, but it is not; in fact, because it's done so well, the method becomes revelatory of the nature of prejudice, all prejudice. It is an effective, and brave, piece of theatrical interpretation.

It's almost unfair to single out members of this true ensemble, because everyone is just fine, but, in terms of pure skill and technique, I especially liked Amy Whitman, a wonderfully versatile and touching actress; Elizabeth Rosen, giving glorious voice to Willa Cather's work; Michael O'Connor, who handles a variety of roles beautifully; Charlie Brown, totally alive and extraordinarily involved in what he's doing - and I'd like to snuggle with him sometime, the cutie; and Deanna Alida, very, very funny in the second act piece "The Psychoanalysis of Edward the Dyke." COMING OUT! takes itself seriously, as any thinking work of theatre must, but the cast and creators obviously know that entertainment is the most effective way to make a point in a theatrical situation. THE FAGGOT could learn a lot from COMING OUT! David Roggensack, using pantomime, story-theatre, and improvisational techniques has directed the cast with imagination, skill, and understanding, getting the best by giving the best. No matter where you live or what you believe, COMING OUT! at the Night House is worth a trip. Call for reservations - 691-7539 - now!

The Gay Life: Cartoon vs. Reality?

By MARTIN DUBERMAN

TWO plays about gay life have recently opened in New York. One, "The Faggot," would seem to have everything going for it—an experienced cast, fine physical facilities at The Truck and Warehouse Theater, and the much-acclaimed talents of composer, lyricist, author Al Carmines. It's more than a failure. It's an affront.

The second play, "Coming Out!", would seem to have everything going against it—a cast of 10, only one of whom has had any professional experience, an unknown author, Jonathan Katz, an untried director, David Roggensack, a rudimentary theater, The Night House at 249 West 18th Street and an agit-prop format that conjures up advance visions of a Chinese ballet in honor of The Grain

---

Martin Duberman, Distinguished Service Professor of History at Lehman College, C.U.N.Y., is also a playwright ("In White America"). His most recent book is "Black Mountain: An Exploration in Community."

Harvest. "Coming Out!" is not a complete success, but its impact is profound.

Much, as always, is in the eye of the beholder. Much—not everything. Admirers of "The Faggot" have told me that, like all belated converts, I've become the truest believer in the (gay liberation) Cause; that I judged "The Faggot" not on its own light-hearted terms, but in accord with some presumed standards of "progressive" politics. Well said! We all need a laugh. And if it happens to be at our own expense, if it confirms the social stereotypes that have made our lives as gay people a laugh a minute, well then, here's to those other light-hearted entertainers: Stepin Fetchit, Charlie Chan and the Bloody Injun. *Self*-exploitation is decidedly preferable to the other brands: *we get* to keep the cash.

So I paid a second visit to "The Faggot," asking for nothing more than a "light-hearted good time." I did laugh hard at two routines, and chuckled at a couple more. The song "Nookie Time" *is* hilarious; vintage Carmines wit. I also laughed a lot at "Fag Hag"; Essie Borden is a (Continued on Page 4)

Poet Walt Whitman
"'Slept' is subject to various interpretations"

The Gay Life: Cartoon vs. Reality?

Continued from Page 1

brilliant comic talent. And though I wondered what the scene about Catherine the Great's *partialismus* to the male horse was doing in a musical about gay life, I fell into the crowded aisle when she sang of "my lover half-centaur—and the other half centaur, too."

If "The Faggot" had stuck to dizzy routines à la "Dames at Sea" or "Little Mary Sunshine," we could casually ignore or enjoy it, chalk it up to a revival of camp consciousness—the gay contribution to the epidemic of nostalgia currently sweeping the land. But it doesn't. It pretends to a kaleidoscopic view of gay life. It insists on treating issues with serious implications for millions of people—and does so in terms of tinkly tunes, perky choreography and cartoon realities. In the process, it trivializes everything it touches—gay love or loneliness, fearful secrecies and open struggles, privatism and politics, problems of age and youth, monogamy and promiscuity, jealousy and devotion.

*

"The Faggot's" cheap parodies will help to perpetuate stereotypes that a serious movement has been attempting to eradicate—at the cost of jobs and apartments, jail sentences and beatings, broken noses and rape. A transvestite in "The Faggot" trills the line, "Revolutions are never good news for queens . . . where everything is permitted, nothing is extraordinary."

Would that we currently faced such an alarming prospect. Would that Carmines had heard another transvestite, Sylvia, bellow her rage at the crowd during the June 24 Gay Pride rally—bellow at gays for their indifference to the plight of those beaten and jailed because of openly insisting on being "extraordinary." Sylvia could have told him that musical caricatures of gay life are not good news for revolutionaries. That it's a little late in the day for cutesy-poo time.

Some specifics on the show's damaging frivolity. Do many gays—for reasons ranging from police harassment· to identity confusion —continue to feel desperate about the quality of their lives? Well, "The Faggot" tells us, "some people just like being desperate." A young man in the musical, with an idiotic smirk as broad as his bow tie, sings to us cheerfully of his devotion to misery; he's joined a group called the Dissenters, pledged to resist *any* current view; he's a charter member of the Passive Caucus of the Gay Activists Alliance; and "whenever endangered by normalcy," he has himself committed to a hospital until his desperation again rises to a satisfying level. "Being desperate is a full-time job," he smilingly concludes —

"With friends like 'The Faggot,' the gay movement needs no enemies"

thereby reducing homosexual anguish to a joke, a reduction that heretofore I thought we could safely rely on the straight world to make.

As for gay domesticity, there is everybody's favorite Picasso painting, Gertrude Stein, and her "helpmate," Alice B. Toklas, everybody's favorite cook. They sing along merrily about the joys of "Ordinary Things"—like corn and beans. Bizarre enough in itself, this cloying view of the shared lives of two remarkable women becomes still more startling when we remember that it was Al Carmines, in his brilliant 1968 musical "In Circles," who once found, with almost magical aptness, the visual and musical equivalents for Stein's subtle, quirky, stylized inventions. In "The Faggot," Carmines has managed to make her sound like Maria von Trapp, thereby raising what is perhaps the evening's only interesting question: "Whatever happened to the Al Carmines of 1968?"

Relentlessly, the show issue-hops. Does aging present special problems for gays in a youth-dominated culture and sub-culture? Yes it does, Carmines answers. Why? Because older people get *bored!* He drapes five of the dreary middle - aged complainers over their habitual bar stools, bleating about "the same old bars, the same old boys, the same old pains, the same old joys." Given their semi-catatonic self-pity, it comes as something of a surprise when they manage to rouse themselves at the entrance of "The New Boy in Town." But they do so only to go through routines of seduction so patently self-degrading and offensive, that our sympathies go out to the New Boy, sadistic little teaser though he is.

"The Faggot" has been called a musical version of "Boys in the Band," but that is a gross injustice to Mart Crowley's once-daring, witty play. Even in its moments of melodramatic self-pity and sentimentality, "Boys" dealt feelingly with real aspects of the then dominant gay life style. "The Faggot" is a smug cartoon version of that *same* style. Seeing it, you'd have no idea that gay life in 1973 is in any way different from what it had been in the '50's—except in the absence of all authentic emotion. Crowley disclosed real pain; Carmines, only unrelieved triviality. With friends like "The Faggot," the gay movement needs no enemies.

*

To gain some understanding of the current mood in the gay community, and of the history of oppression that has led up to it, one must see "Coming Out!" The play's achievements are sufficiently honorable and substantial to make extravagant claims in its behalf unnecessary. It is not a theatrical or literary milestone. Its importance is as a political artifact, not art—the difference between exemplifying a historical moment and creating one. Nor do the modest people connected with the show pretend to anything more grandiloquent. They wish to inform and energize, to testify to past griefs and to provide an instrument for future struggle.

*

From old journals and police records, autobiographies and novels, legislative reports and letters, newspaper accounts and poems, Jonathan Katz, the author, has fashioned a "documentary history about gay life and liberation in the U.S.A." It has not been a history easy to come by. If there are few blacks or women in our textbooks, there are no gays. The standard works on even celebrated literary figures (Gay Wilson Allen's biography of Walt Whitman, for example, or Leon Edel's "Henry James") demurely bypass the question of sexual preference, presuming no more than an occasional elevated "infatuation." But the presumption of *sex?*—Never! No one in our history, it seems, has ever been to bed with anybody of the same gender—certainly no one of stature or accomplishment.

*

Yet Jonathan Katz has collected evidence to the contrary—including three entries from Walt Whitman's 1862 notebooks in the Library of Congress, one of them a charming reference to 19-year-old David Wilson, who worked in a blacksmith's shop. Whitman says that he slept with him. "Slept," to be sure, is subject to various interpretations; our scholars may yet be able to rescue Walt from the ghastly imputation of carnal knowledge, preferring to burden him instead with what has been called the one true sexual aberration: chastity.

Katz has also gathered abundant horror stories to document our country's insistent homo-phobia through time. They range from the 17th-century execution (by choking) of a black slave who had committed sodomy, to Diego Vinales impaled three years ago on the spikes of an iron fence, after he tried to jump from a second-story window in police headquarters where he had been brought following a raid on a gay bar. Some of the play's recent material makes clear that the oppressed, in increasing numbers, have stopped internalizing the guilt long inculcated by the society. The horror show is ending: because this generation has a different definition of what constitutes criminal behavior—not love or honest lust, but napalming babies, betraying friends, proscribing human diversity.

Though "Coming Out!" details a bitter history of social stigmatization and private shame, it also contains hilarious and cleansing humor. "The Psychoanalysis of Edward the Dyke," written by Judy Grahn and performed with twinkling gusto by Deanna Alida, provides more gut laughs in 10 minutes than "The Faggot" does in two hours. And it's the laughter of survival, not self-betrayal.

The second act of "Coming Out!" needs cutting. Although the director, David Roggensack, has shrewdly encouraged the cast to utilize the emotional resources of their own experience as gay people, passion does not always compensate for lack of technique. At times the pacing is too quick — the gulps were still in my throat after Diego Vinales's moving words about his continuing dream of "a good life in America," when I was rushed away to another setting and mood.

I could have done with fewer moral strictures against "mating like dogs in heat" and more celebration of erotic pleasure — though Roggensack's direction skillfully "physicalizes" the material whenever feasible. And I would have liked more on bi-sexuality — that is, less about gay versus straight, and more on the dawning possibilities of being gay and straight.

So, "Coming Out!" isn't everything. But it is a lot. To the extent that history (personal and collective) helps to provide the basis for identity, this documentary gives the gay movement substantial materials with which to build—and the straight world, substantial insights into the necessity for the movement. Gay and straight alike will profit infinitely more (at half the price) from a viewing of "Coming Out!" than from "The Faggot."

The one deals in lives, the other in stereotypes. The one stirs, the other lulls. The one provides a context for struggle, the other an excuse for ignoring it. The one suggests the need for unity and commitment, the other for bikinis and cocktails. The one demands an end to oppression, the other helps to reinforce it. Where "The Faggot" is a belated memento of the older view of gay self-deprecation, "Coming Out!" marks the moment when "a yes has come into it."

'Politics Is Not Art'

To the Editor:

IN responding to Martin Duberman's broadside attack on my musical play, "The Faggot," let me first say that I have both respect and affection for him — not only for his superb documentary theater piece, "In White America," but also for the kind words he has had for my work in the past. I also respect and think I agree with his stand on gay liberation and I admire his forthrightness and the enormous sense of compassion which emerges from his article in The Times of July 22, "The Gay Life: Cartoon vs. Reality?"

However, although I agree with Mr. Duberman's political position regarding gay liberation, in the case of "The Faggot" he is not dealing with a political position paper, but rather with a personal, idiosyncratic, quirky, highly subjective theater piece. This is the crux of the disagreement between Mr. Duberman and myself. I do not believe politics is art and I believe a confusion of those two human activities is a dangerous and ultimately catastrophic misunderstanding.

*

Mr. Duberman is really accusing me of not being politically acute in "The Faggot." To this I plead guilty. I plead guilty because I believe it is precisely this obsession with political models that is the bane of American life today and the bane of its liberation movements.

Politics is finally a concern with strategy — the use of certain facts or images to gain a desired end. I believe that strategy has nothing at all to do with art. I am not concerned with the "image" gay people or straight people would like to project. If I wanted to deal in those images, I would be in advertising, not theater. However my work offends Mr. Duberman, I can assure him that there are four questions I did not ask in writing "The Faggot":

(1) How will "The Faggot" affect the gay community?

(2) Does it adequately explain the gay life to "straights"?

(3) Does it help the gay cause?

(4) Is it politically liberated and correct?

No, Mr. Duberman, these are questions I did not ask and, if I had asked them, I would consider myself unworthy to aspire to the name of artist.

I spent five years in a theological seminary filled with earnest young men and women who believed that *their* earnestness was sufficient redemption for the world. Therefore, I am afraid that I am inoculated against the kind of seriousness that is more concerned with doing what is politically correct than with what is quick with life and truth. My domain—if I have one—is that crack between ideologies where contradictory, frustrating, unideological, stinking and thrilling humanity raises its head.

My drag queen in "The Faggot" is not a representative drag queen. She is an individual with no causes to espouse except her own unshakable existence My desperation dancer is not concerned that his desperation seems slighting to Mr. Duberman's sexual ideology. He is telling the story of one life —his own. My bored and depressed middle-aged homosexuals are not interested in pretending that they are *not* bored and depressed middle-aged homosexuals in order to gild the image of gay liberation. In short, Mr. Duberman, my characters are themselves with their and my very personal pain and joy in relating to this world.

*

No matter how benign, no matter how humanitarian, no matter how compassionate, no matter how just, those who would have any artist trim his vision to fit a sociological or political need for the "right things being said" are the corrupters of art. As a political entity, I am committed to gay liberation and many other liberations. As an artist, I am committed only to the absolute human truth as I see it. And that truth is far more complicated than any party line, however noble, could ever be.

Mr. Duberman asks where the Al Carmines of 1968 is. In 1968, Mr. Duberman, I wrote only music. And I used music to underline, accentuate and, I am afraid, occasionally undercut the lyrics of those with whom I wrote. I did not write words because I was intimidated by people like you, Mr. Duberman — people sheathed in a point of view like heavy armor. And then I discovered that I, too, had a point of view — a shriek against all

Al Carmines
"I'd rather be Herblock than Max Lerner"

those causes that demanded blind commitment and that certain messy facts can be conveniently left out if they blur the desired image.

I do not believe that, because gays have suffered, they are perfect. I do not believe that, because we struggle, we cannot laugh at ourselves. And I do not believe that gays, as well as everyone else, have to deal with self - glorification, self - righteousness and pomposity. I write of both the squalor and the glory of homosexuality, of both the confusion and the clarity; of both the ludicrousness and the holiness of the sexual life.

I have spent a lifetime trying to see what I see — rather than what leftists, rightists, gays, straights, old or young tell me I *ought* to see. I don't believe the only acceptable plays about homosexuality are those which wallow in self-pity or sound the call to arms. I believe there are ways of being black, or a woman, or gay, or anything else which are not comprehended in even your compassionate militancy, Mr. Duberman.

As for the accusation that "The Faggot" deals with serious issues in terms of "cartoon realities," well, yes— if given the choice, I would rather be Herblock than Max Lerner. And that, perhaps, is the real difference between Mr. Duberman and myself.   Al Carmines
New York City

Furor Over 'The Faggot'

TO THE EDITOR:

I WOULD like to comment on Al Carmines's response to Martin Duberman's review of Carmine's "The Faggot" and my own play, "Coming Out!" (July 29, 1973). The Duberman-Carmines debate raises publicly for the first time some basic questions about a new, developing gay culture; the answers will affect its future character.

Carmines assumes an absolute opposition between politics and art, coming down totally on the side of "art" —an ivory-tower view I believed had gone out with the glorious 1950's. I thought we were all agreed by now that there is a necessary and intimate interconnection between such formerly disparate "fields" as art, sexuality, and politics.

Carmines seems to think his play is not political or ideological. In fact, "The Faggot" could not even have reached Off Broadway, much less be advertised in the subways, if the militant gay liberation struggles of recent years had not forced Americans to consider that previously unmentionable subject.

"The Faggot" is also political in that it adds to the oppression of gays; it trivializes our experience and reinforces stereotypes, as well as failing to indicate any of the social pressures which have led to homosexual self-hate and desperation.

Carmines explicitly states that he does not care what effect his play has on straights or the gay community or liberation movement. From his position on high, "artist" Carmines will not stoop to such work-a-day concerns. In this context, Carmines's lip service "to gay liberation and many other liberations" sounds like empty liberal rhetoric. The Rev. Carmines's elitest, art-for-art's- sake philosophy, by denying the social and *human* effect of his art, is finally irresponsible.

I do not feel there is any antagonism between the artistic and the political. I find most exciting that art which is explicitly political and engaged and, yes, highly creative, an art which is an act of defiance against a society oppressive to gays, women, blacks, American Indians, orientals, old people, young people, working people, etc., etc.

There exists at this particular time in our history what seems to me a marvelously inspiring and challenging role for the homosexual artist: to create a new, liberated gay culture which is both of high artistic quality and reflective of the new consciousness being created by gay liberationists. While there is certainly room and necessity for many kinds of gay art, I hope that more gay culture will come to embody this new gay awareness, including a sense of the social situation of homosexuals, anger at our oppression, and joyous self-affirmation.

JONATHAN KATZ
New York City.

"INTEGRITY"

TO THE EDITOR:

Al Carmines's response to Martin Duberman is a fine statement of what it means to be an artist.

Carmines—an independent, an outlaw, a rebel, call him what you may — is fighting for the integrity of his soul, if I may use an old-fashioned word. In essence, he is saying, "World, capitalism, little people and big, don't break my critical canons—as a man and as an artist."

LUCAS LONGO
New Haven, Conn.

"COMPLEX SUBJECT"

TO THE EDITOR:

Martin Duberman complains that there are no "gays" in our textbooks: "The standard works on even celebrated literary figures (Gay Wilson Allen's biography of Walt Whitman, for example, or Leon Edel's 'Henry James') demurely bypass the question of sexual preference, presuming no more than an occasional elevated 'infatuation.' But the presumption of sex?—Never! No one in our history, it seems, has ever been to bed with anybody of the same gender. . ."

Evidently Professor Duberman has not read my biography of Whitman with much attention (or Edel's later volumes of "Henry James" either), for in numerous places I discuss Whitman's deep homoerotic emotions. But I did not detail all the men the poet "slept" with, or state that he slept with them to engage in sodomy. That he may have I nowhere denied, but no detective broke into the room to record the act, and for all I *actually* know he may have shared beds because the beds he could afford were scarce. I think a biographer should go as far as his facts permit, but not to state as positive truth what took place in the dark of night without more evidence than Whitman's ambiguous words "slept with" —even Duberman admits the ambiguity.

Perhaps in 1973 it is fatuous to insist on a difference between physical sexuality and fantasy, especially for those who think that to be called "gay" is an honor. In 1955, when I published the Whitman biography, the term was not publicly sought, yet if I were writing the book today I would not handle Whitman's sex pathology differently. And I would still try to avoid simplifying a complex subject, for Whitman was not consistently a textbook example of a homosexual — perhaps no one is. My only regret is that when I began publishing I could not foresee that 40 years later my first name would become an acute embarrassment.

GAY WILSON ALLEN
Oradell, N.J.

"SHORTSIGHTED"

TO THE EDITOR:

I find Martin Duberman's review of Al Carmines' "The Faggot" lamentably shortsighted; what he fails to grasp is Carmines' idea that the best way of getting beyond homosexual stereotypes is not by ignoring them but by exploding them.

Carmines breaks through, with humor and lyric sensibility, those very clichés he sets up and, the audience, rather than being put down by the experience, is permitted a reshuffling of the cliché-cards, and therefore a new awareness.

Duberman does both the audience and the gay movement a disservice when he confuses the solemnity of gay rhetoric with gay pride, and thinks of laughter as the enemy.

MICHAEL GRUMLEY
New York City

"POLITICIZED"

TO THE EDITOR:

How, in the midst of the dynamic social, political and sexual revolution, no less, the gay movement, which is germinating all around us, does Al Carmines presume to be liberated without being politicized?

As Jonathan Katz's "Coming Out!" clearly indicates, and Martin Duberman's political sensitivity reveals, being gay should presently connote explicit articulation and action in regard to the phenomenon of gay oppression. Liberation means having your head and body together and in concert with gay brothers and sisters undertaking the very psychological and political creation of gay actualization.

Carmines might profit from a scrutiny of the life and works of the most successful song and dance man of the modern theater — Bertolt Brecht, the totally politicized man and playwright.

DR. FRANK S. GALASSI
Asst. Professor of Theater,
Borough of Manhattan
Community College
Brooklyn, N. Y.

"UNSATISFYING"

TO THE EDITOR:

Not only must a theatrical work about gay life staged in 1973 necessarily have a political dimension, it must even have political consequences because of its effect on a large audience. The dimension here is the negative one of omission. If you don't challenge the present view of homosexuals, you reinforce it.

"The Faggot" is unsatisfying not because it's totally inaccurate but because it's incomplete. No one doubts that many homosexuals are miserable or bored, and no one asks to see a fake, projected image of the happy, problemless homosexual as a theatrical subject. However, it is disappointing that Carmines is willing to leave out the most significant scenes in his panorama of the gay experience, those encounters which show why many homosexuals have become accustomed to despair.

ALFRED CORN
New York City

"FUNCTION OF ARTS"

TO THE EDITOR:

While I disagree with Al Carmine's apparently blanket dichotomy between "art" and "politics," I also disagree with Martin Duberman's suggestion that, when drama transforms human oppression into a circus, it loses its political punch and moreover becomes crassly insensitive to human pain.

The clown is both a comic and a tragic figure. We laugh at him, or her; and maybe in laughing, we hide our tears. Perhaps it's because we are the clown — gay, straight, rich, poor, black, white, brown, male, or female. And because we can't quite deal with the reality of the tragic. It's been said that humankind can bear but so much reality. A function of art is sometimes to help us get as close to the reality as we, the audience, can — and then to leave us, suspended with our own consciences and capacities, by which we determine the next move.

(The Rev.) CARTER HEYWARD
Union Theological Seminary
New York City

Gay Liberation Play Urges Political Power

BY BRUCE HUSTEN

ALBANY—Political power is the only route the Gay Liberation movement can hope to travel and attain the goals it seeks.

This was the message the original New York cast of "Coming Out" brought to a full house Wednesday in Draper Hall of Albany State University.

"We're just like Negroes and Jews and women. We want our rights." "We no longer have the energy to hide." "The cure for homosexuality is rebellion. "We won't have our rights until we use our power."

Such is the dogmatic propaganda espoused by the 10 gay cast members of the play that has been selling out since June at The Night House in Greenwich Village The one-night Albany performance was sponsored by the Gay Alliance of Albany State University.

Jonatham Katz' script, billed as "a documentary play about gay life and liberation in the U.S.A.," is something of a crossbeed between theater and blatant rhetoric.

It has, in fact, been the subject of some artistic controversy in New York since another gay play of an entirely different breed — "The Faggot" by Al Carmines — has opened to rival it.

To look at the two plays is to look at the plight of the homosexual movement in America today, torn as it is right down the middle.

On the "Coming Out" side, you've got the liberated gays trying to turn the cause into political power movement, urging gay brothers and sisters to "come out of the closet" and declare their state of body and mind.

On the "Faggot" side, you've got the mincing, limp-wristed fairies, living up to the caricatures that have been created for homosexuals from the day one.

"The movement" is so factionalized down the middle that it is likely to get nowhere until the one can overcome the other.

The question that has been raised in New York is not whether the movement needs the political element of the "Coming Out" faction, but rather whether that element has to be brought into the theater and presented with the facade of art.

After seeing "Coming Out," however, there can be no falling for that argument, for the "play" never really intends to be artistic.

From Walt Hitman, Gertrude Stein and Alice B. Toklas to Alan Ginsburg, Merle Miller and Kate Millett, "Comong Out" traces the history of repressed and liberated homosexuals and makes a pungent case for the necessity of a power struggle.

This is no plea to the straight world for acceptance; it is, rather, a confident statement of brotherhood to the gays and a blatant threat of violent aggression to the straights. "This is no fairy tale," one of the all-gay cast members announced. "The sound of silence will be replaced by the sounds of sirens."

And, according to director David Roggensack, "Coming Out" has been achieving its goals. "A lot of gay people have to come over to me after the play and told me they agree and a lot of other 'closet cases' have told me the play inspired them to come out of the closet." Even some straight people, Roggensack said, have been moved to acceptance by the play.

And while the production as staged in Albany was plagued by repeated blackouts, a tiny stage, and an audience sweltering from the lack of air-conditioning, "Coming Out" got its message across.

After a decade of American Negroes fighting against the rightness of whiteness, it seems it's now the homosexual's turn to fight against the greatness of straightness.

On "Coming Out"

by Nancy Miller

Undaunted by the oppressive heat and a blackout which necessitated the viewing of the second act by lantern light, the Coming Out Collective presented a two-hour play entitled "Coming Out," to a full house at Draper Hall last Wednesday night. Billed as a "documentary play about gay life and liberation in the U.S.A.," author Jonathan Katz has largely succeeded in his goal by compiling an impressive array of quotes, anecdotes, and autobiographical accounts to dramatize the gay experience in America.

Seeking to provide a context in which to view the gay liberation movement, "Coming Out" records the abuses brought to bear on homosexuals in this country. Beginning with the dramatization of the execution of a seventeenth century slave for the commission of sodomy, and continuing up to present day persecution best illustrated by the Snake Pit Raid (1970) which ended tragically when Diego Vanales leapt to his death from a police headquarters window following his arrest in a raid on a gay bar, the play becomes a vehicle wherein the frustrations and prejudices which have characterized the gay experience are aired and exosed for what they are. In an effort to document both the contributions made by gay authors as well as to trace the various representations of gay life in literature, Katz draws from the novels, poetry, and diaries of such people as Willa Cather, Sherwood Anderson, Walt Whitman, and Gertrude Stein.

Taken together, these stories and pieces paint a painful and sometimes bitter portrait of the struggle to forge a gay identity, and these are offset (with good results) by lighter, more humorous treatments of the same material. The most effective of these was "The Psychoanalysis of Edward the Dyke" in which Deanna Alida shines in the title role.

Opening with the innocent revelation to the analyst, "As soon as I explained that I was a harmless dyke the trouble began," the sketch proceeds in an uproarious fashion building up the momentum which culminates in the "March and Gay-In," at the conclusion of the play.

Although the play was presented in less than optimum conditions (the blackout notwithstanding), the performance was uneven in spots with the second act much better paced than the first. But what may have been lacking in finesse was compensated for by the players' enthusiasm and conviction in what they were doing. In addition to Deanna Alida, Elizabeth Rosen and Michael O'Connor were also particularly effective.

The value of "Coming Out" is not, however, primarily as a theatrical piece, but in its expression of the bitterness and resentment and the hopes and aspirations of homosexuals in the U.S. Its acceptance and approval (both as a play and in its wider socio-political implications) was signalled by the chant of G-A-Y P-O-W-E-R which was begun in the gay-in and was supplemented by members of the audience. One leaves with the sense that the process of "Coming Out" as a force quite apart from the play is not only *not* ending, but, on the contrary, is just beginning.

win

September 13, 1973   Volume IX, No. 26

REVIEWS

Dempster Leach as the male chavinist peasant, Wang, in "The Women's Representative", a Chinese play by Sun Yu.

THE WOMAN'S REPRESENTATIVE
Sun Yu, adaptation by David Gaard
directed by Pamela de Sio, presented by M. Sanford Kaplan and Mr. Gaard—at 8:30 P.M. Tuesdays and Wednesdays and 10:30 P.M. Fridays and Saturdays at the Night House, 249 West 18th Street, New York City

COMING OUT!
Jonathan Katz
directed by David Rogensack, sponsored by the Gay Activist Alliance, Thursdays at 8:30 P.M., Fridays to Sundays at 7:30 P.M. at the Night House.

By coincidence I saw both these plays for purposes of reviewing them on the same evening. They are playing in tandem at the same theater, the Night House, and perhaps that is all that they share. But they feel like they should be reviewed together. One, Coming Out, deals with homo-sexuality in past and present America. The other, The Woman's Representative, with male chauvinism in present-day China. Both have a stab at explaining something about important questions in their respective societies. Both are highly propagandistic. Both are deeply satisfying, I suppose, if you agree with their basic premises, both somewhat boring if you don't. Both seem to preach to the converted.

The Woman's Representative, we are told in the program, won for its authoress the 1953 People's Playwriting Contest in China. Well, judging by this work, the people weren't writing very good plays in the early 50's in China. A great deal of care has been lavished by director Pamela de Sio and her very talented cast on what is probably the most simplistic, brittle, thinly fabricated, predictable and plain boring piece of propaganda it has ever been my experience to sit through in the theater.

The play is about a male chauvinist peasant, Wang, who returns home from a trip to a far off market to find his wife has learned to do mathematics, is learning to read, is instrum-

ental in a literacy campaign for the village women, has been elected her village's woman representative to the political councils and is already pulling political strings around town. Now that is a heap to happen while one is off trying to get a decent price for a few hogs, and Wang reacts by trying to batten down the hatches of control that were so safely closed when he left. Though he wields a whip and blusters like a character more out of Chekov's Russian than Mao's China, Wang is finally quelled by his wife. In fact, by play's end, I would say she's so turned the tables on her husband that she is well on her way toward becoming a female chauvinist sow but that's a personal opinion and hardly substantiated by anything intended by the playwright.

Of course, the odds are rather stacked against Wang from the start. Besides a wife who will no doubt rise to the Chairmanship of the Chinese Communist party or at least head China's nuclear weapons program before the decade is out, the poor peasant must contend with his own proverb-spouting mother (the Chinese version of the Jewish Mother I should say); Aunt Niu, the meddlesome neighbor to end all meddlesome neighbors; and a little female leftover from the Cultural Revolution who could drive Confucious nuts in the time it takes to open your little red book. Old Wang hasn't a Chinaman's chance, if you'll pardon the expression.

The interesting thing about this production is the superb acting. Dempster Leech as the male chauvinist peasant made much of a pretty stupid part. And Roberta Pikser as Aunt Niu, the neighbor, could find laughs in a lemon. Ellen Schindler as Wang's mother had most of the evening's best lines, unintended by the author I'm sure. Her best Chinese chestnut: "It is the best talker who suffers most." That probably sums up most of the political problems of the Gainsville Eight, Jerry Rubin and most of the rest of us.

The costumes and setting by Timothy Miles were colorful and fun and, I suspect, nearer the Mikado than Mao. But they served to liven a wooden play that needed all the life it could get.

Although I agreed with the Woman's Lib. message of the play, I was alternately horrified, angered and finally just plain bored with the empty propagandistic technique of the writing. It sounded like the playwright faced a prison term if she didn't please the censors and she wasn't about to chance spending one second behind bars for her art. If this is any example of the depth in which social problems are treated by the contemporary Chinese theater, then what a deadly dull business going to the theater there must be. But perhaps things have improved since the early 1950's.

In contrast to the Chinese torture is the other play currently playing at the Night House, Coming Out! It is basically an agit-prop. piece on Gay Liberation. It is an attempt to convey some of the Gay experience and foster Gay pride through the writing and speaking of Gay personalities. Everyone you might expect to hear from is there. There are cuts from Walt Whitman and Gertrude Stein. There is David McReynolds culled from the pages of WIN Magazine in one of the evening's most moving moments defiantly proclaiming his radical politics and his homosexuality. But the name dropping gets somehow repetitious. And although you don't remember the quotes exactly, and probably haven't really heard many of them before, they have an over-familiar ring to them. One hungers for some calm, honest talk from somebody you never heard of before which might enlighten a corner of Gay experience. The show could use a little less of the rhetoric which treads so heavily over basically well-traveled ground. The tone eventually becomes yelling, the raised consciousnesses become bullying harangues, and author Jonathan's Katz's attempt to instill Gay pride in his

What the obvious direction and often clumsy cast do give, however, is a terribly convincing feeling of commitment. And it makes this an amateur production in the *best* sense of the word. Everyone is up there because they believe in what they are saying and doing and because they must make these ideas known to a wider world. This is in itself powerfully moving. However tedious the tone of the show sometimes was for me, I do know that many people around me were deeply affected. I know that for many people, this will be the first time in their lives that they will have seen what they feel and believe stomped and shouted from a stage. This is tremendously important and it is very exciting to witness. I don't think I have ever had a theater experience quite like this and I suspect there is nothing to compare with it in New York.

Picked up by a good college theater group or a more experienced professional company, **Coming Out** may even prove to be a pretty skillful compiling of the thoughts and feelings of those gays with the courage and the forum to speak out about their loves and their lot.   — Lance Belville

audience becomes something akin to eating an over-spiced taco: all fire without much flavor. Pride in what one is and must be is something more and deeper than screaming, fist-shaking defiance. Somehow old Walt Whitman comes off as almost the only calm human being with loves and a humanistic point of view amid all those tough, belligerent gays. Not that gay life and art haven't the right, indeed the necessity, to be pretty tough and sometimes belligerent, but two hours of it is hard to take when you're a straight and the theater is hot and crowded.

In fairness to Katz's script, I should point out that the actors are inexperienced and totally committed to their work, a combination that hardly leads to sensitive, deep-toned performances. And probably director David Rogensack must take some of the blame for the bombastic acting. His blocking, which is a sort of semi-choreographed miming, unfailingly goes for the most obvious in the spoken text and allows inexperienced actors to do what comes most naturally to them: over acting, sometimes horrendous, even in this amateur context.

Photos on this page by Bettye Lane: The cast in scenes from "Coming Out!" a play by Jonathan Katz.

HOMOSEXUALITY

Lesbians and Gay Men
in Society, History and Literature

Acosta, Mercedes de. **Here Lies The Heart.** 1960

Bannon, Ann. **I Am a Woman.** 1959

Bannon, Ann. **Journey To a Woman.** 1960

Bannon, Ann. **Odd Girl Out.** 1957

Bannon, Ann. **Women in The Shadows.** 1959

Barney, Natalie Clifford. **Aventures de L'Esprit.** 1929

Barney, Natalie Clifford. **Traits et Portraits.** 1963

Brooks, Romaine. **Portraits, Tableaux, Dessins.** 1952

Carpenter, Edward. **Intermediate Types Among Primitive Folk.** 1919

Casal, Mary. **The Stone Wall.** 1930

Cory, Donald Webster. **The Homosexual in America.** 1951

Craigin, Elisabeth. **Either Is Love.** 1937

Daughters of Bilitis. **The Ladder.** Volumes I - XVI. Including an **Index To The Ladder** by Gene Damon. 1956 - 1972. Nine vols.

Documents of the Homosexual Rights Movement in Germany, 1836 - 1927. 1975

Ellis, Havelock and John Addington Symonds. **Sexual Inversion.** 1897

Fitzroy, A. T. **Despised and Rejected.** 1917

Ford, Charles and Parker Tyler. **The Young and Evil.** 1933

Frederics, Diana. **Diana: A Strange Autobiography.** 1939

Friedlaender, Benedict. **Renaissance des Eros Uranios.** 1904

A Gay Bibliography. 1975

A Gay News Chronology, 1969 - May, 1975. 1975

Gordon, Mary. **Chase of the Wild Goose.** 1936

Government Versus Homosexuals. 1975

Grosskurth, Phyllis. **John Addington Symonds.** 1964

Gunn, Peter. **Vernon Lee: Violet Paget, 1856 - 1935.** 1964

A Homosexual Emancipation Miscellany, c. 1835 - 1952. 1975

Karsch-Haack, F[erdinand]. **Das Gleichgeschlechtliche Leben der Naturvölker.** 1911

Katz, Jonathan. **Coming Out!** 1975

Lesbianism and Feminism in Germany, 1895 - 1910. 1975

Lind, Earl. **Autobiography of an Androgyne.** 1918

Lind, Earl. **The Female-Impersonators.** 1922

Loeffler, Donald L. **An Analysis of the Treatment of the Homosexual Character in Dramas Produced in the New York Theatre From 1950 to 1968.** 1975

Mallet, Françoise. **The Illusionist.** 1952

Miss Marianne Woods and Miss Jane Pirie Against Dame Helen Cumming Gordon. 1811 - 1819

Mattachine Society. **Mattachine Review.** Volumes I - XIII. 1955 - 1966. Six vols.

Mayne, Xavier. **Imre: A Memorandum.** 1908

Mayne, Xavier. **The Intersexes.** 1908

Morgan, Claire. **The Price of Salt.** 1952

Niles, Blair. **Strange Brother.** 1931

Olivia. **Olivia.** 1949

Rule, Jane. **The Desert of the Heart.** 1964

Sagarin, Edward. **Structure and Ideology in an Association of Deviants.** 1975

Steakley, James D. **The Homosexual Emancipation Movement in Germany.** 1975

Sturgeon, Mary C. **Michael Field.** 1921

Sutherland, Alistair and Patrick Anderson. **Eros: An Anthology of Friendship.** 1961

Sweet, Roxanna Thayer. **Political and Social Action in Homophile Organizations.** 1975

Tobin, Kay and Randy Wicker. **The Gay Crusaders.** 1972

Ulrichs, Carl Heinrich. **Forschungen Über Das Rätsel Der Mannmännlichen Liebe.** 1898

Underwood, Reginald. **Bachelor's Hall.** 1937

[Vincenzo], Una, Lady Troubridge. **The Life of Radclyffe Hall.** 1963

Vivien, Renée **Poèmes de Renée Vivien.** Two vols. in one. 1923/24

Weirauch, Anna Elisabet. **The Outcast.** 1933

Weirauch, Anna Elisabet. **The Scorpion.** 1932

Wilhelm, Gale. **Torchlight to Valhalla.** 1938

Wilhelm, Gale. **We Too Are Drifting.** 1935

Winsloe, Christa. **The Child Manuela.** 1933

ACB 1264

4/30/90

PS
3561
A 756
C6
1975

0 00 02 0482411 4
MIDDLEBURY COLLEGE